Daniel Lamboy is a New Jersey born, Michigan raised, Cuban/Puerto Rican aspiring writer. He has a penchant for poetry with darker topics and themes. While he never expected *The Fume of Fresh Ash* to be published, he hopes his readers enjoy reading it as much as he enjoyed writing it.

To a number of people I was lucky enough to find in this odd little life I'm living.

Daniel Lamboy

THE FUME OF FRESH ASH

AUSTIN MACAULEY PUBLISHERS™

LONDON • CAMBRIDGE • NEW YORK • SHARJAH

Copyright © Daniel Lamboy (2020)

Ordering Information:
Quantity sales: special discounts are available on quantity purchases by corporations, associations, and others. For details, contact the publisher at the address below.

Publisher's Cataloging-in-Publication data
Lamboy, Daniel
The Fume of Fresh Ash

ISBN 9781643786872 (Paperback)
ISBN 9781643786889 (Hardback)
ISBN 9781645364863 (ePub e-book)

Library of Congress Control Number: 2019919327

www.austinmacauley.com/us

First Published (2020)
Austin Macauley Publishers LLC
40 Wall Street, 28th Floor
New York, NY 10005
USA

mail-usa@austinmacauley.com
+1 (646) 5125767

I'd like to say thank you to the publisher, the editors, to everyone who helped put this on shelves, and whoever decides to read this. This one goes out for the friends I kept up talking about anything under the sun, my parents, and the teachers who gave me the confidence to keep writing.

1

The bulking behemoth
A shadowy colossus shadily staring like a fierce hawk
Eyes of glowing rage and toxins
Dead set on bringing down a holy flail
And repaint the cheap plaster cell
Rubbing off old paint with salted teary streaks
To apply the crimson sheets along each edge.

A cursed crusade cast upon a child
Lashings and bruises to kill a crowd
Bringing down a hammer to collide as another sheet
Another layer to smear for this godless gory scene of a
madman's rage
As who would bite the hand that feeds
Even if its meat is poisoned and rotten
A decomposed cow is a cruel meat
With naught but flesh and decay as a topping.

Then to take it all away
Every bite, every morsel
Awaiting a pursuit of polishing ego
With a starving slave dying from fierce lashings

Leaving another dead on the floor
Letting the next victim of his iron hand
Rise to smite him and topple his throne
Taking a stained crown of cursed crimson.

2

The risen man
One of loss, pain, and whaling throughout thick nights
With a lover dead, lacerated and buried
And a father ripe for disposal
Wrapped in a pitch black dream
A David for a demonic goliath
Set on an answer of agonizing red
Justice served on the head of an ashen spear
Or a cloudy gun where clouds have since perished
A cracked crying cackle with a finished deed.

A putrid scent and stain begrudgingly remains
A man's filth and grimy generosities
An illusion seeking pathologic falsehood
Dead set on murderous intent.
Screeching for a monster to take him to the ground
A ferocious fool and a mad jester
But oh, how the lines blur
Laughing away angrily in awful anguish
All sharpened and polished
Not another statement, but a wish

Death is knocking on his door on another's pitch black shoulders
Ready to blow as the click is heard.

Another fool in irons
Though this one is sympathetic
Serving a sentence for a shivering stay
Clicking and clacking, too scared for parole
To stain a fate in a pinewood box
Covered in dirt and rock, below an unmarked grave beside a lost love
But who, dare I ask,
Would bear a son's pain?
As pitch black stained the gene pool
And a saddened shovel finishes its work, daring a rising sun.

3

A case too easy to close
Oddity strikes the justifying jury
As another cry reigns supreme
A beast slain, gifting another its blood and bile,
And a jet-set soul with a bloodied face
The guilt of a murderous man's demise
By once innocent hands of stained soot
Summed up in palms dripping cool crimson
And a son left to his uncle's detached hand
To be fed and needs met but naught else.

A Father's dead lover
His last home will be an inferno
A righteous job but a blazing sentence
Teary years locked away.
For a life thought pure,
Purposefully left purposeless even among pews
Repent will burn such a wicked soul.

His fate stained, sealed and locked
After an attempt to glide with sheets
Tightly grouped together in a looped chain

To grasp a final, soaring, foolish thought
And burned by solely his young
Set upon by a pitch black blaze
A life destined for trails and trials
Living in the shadow of a damned righteous jester
Bojangles, and all left to rot
Even after all those years
Father remembers Son
And the box creaks open once more.

4

Light rain first
Then reins handed back
To a righteous sinner rising
On a pitch black night
Only a pale moonlight to bounce on baby's flesh
A father reborn as the dancing devil
Laughing and swaying as life is in his hands.

After years of stale flame
Fleeing and returning corporeal
Accepting to his cruel fate
To guide a scarred son
Both stained by the mother's death
She was his precious lover
And the child was much too young.

On the curse from a modest visit
Death and scars for the three
Now the fatherly newborn is newly born
Rot resting in a horrid dealer's tomb
Gifting the purposeless man with purposeful breath and
gems

Twin glistening rubies accustomed to a focused stare
Left to wander, lost and afraid
Until stumbling across a weathered wintery home
Missing the dirt of the dreary spring's death
And knocking at the door
Awaiting a bitter reunion
Onwards to a sweet victory.

5

Home, back and it fits like a glove
But it's so much dirtier than I remember
A dark new shadow resonating along each crack and seam
Seemingly, where it all began
Sitting on that same old sofa
Sliding down in my old groove
Where so long ago I sharpened my sadness
Preparing to pierce a purposeful poisonous heart.

A man walks into my inherited home
Skin pale with dazzling crimson eyes
A dead set man, but with oddly youthful skin
A layer of mud, a grimy black suit
Yet worn as if for years
Fiddling with sleeve ends who could this man be.

A son in an empty home
That I've only seen in absent-minded dreams
Dusty full of sublime memories
Whisking me back into her arms
And dancing the night away in the living room
Knocking over chairs in a semi-drunken haze

Laughing before exhaustion took its debt
Falling upon once soft cushions
The sloppy and sweet of a night that I once lived.

A father absent for so many years
I was three at his demise
I buried him deep inside hoping to forget, yet I can't cast
him aside
Back once again to sweep my mind away
Once I thought that I could be sane
But now that I see pitch black rubies
And another starless sky
I shiver and shake at the sinister man sitting in front of me
While there's blood on his hands being delicately wiped
off.

We can see that nothing will be the same
He's terrified by the man that crawled from the grave
Sprawling on an old stained couch
With a handkerchief draped on an old wine glass
Dipped in the little liquid and stained on the fallen side
To stale along another night.

6

The end was all a lie
And though death do us part
I lay here dead set on finding you again
Even if I have to lacerate more flesh
Laying a fine gilded mesh and mess for the world
Till death do us part
And the dates all blend on a vanilla sky
Wishing for it to rain once more
Reflecting on your face
Now flat and stone.

How many murals will I paint
Without using those brushes or daint?
Flimsy tools there until I faint
But yet again I will rise
With crimson hands for ruby eyes
Sparkling along with starless skies
As empty to as the gaze I loved
The one I remember throughout this inky dream
With my hazy view until focus brings back life

To splattered red while heads roll for more
Kicking down the pearly gates
Burning away this earthly prison.

These new eyes haunt me
The remnants of a trickster who told me terrors and truths
But lied about wings to soar back to your side
Yet I burn this trail
Flames will be my guide to solace and skies
Blazing through fields of foolish flesh
Watching the ashes and embers
Before I'm trapped in an urn
A desert's grey blizzard
But will I paint the flakes red
When my hands slip from sweat and grease
As the first is felled through a bloody crusade
Laughing away the night with cold steel as my cruel
partner
My life for the crimson pool.

7

All those years ago
When the crusade was changing hands
Gunshots at the door and a wounded stomach
To then be dragged across a table
The clattering of cheap china cutting into shoes and souls
While scarlet hands reach to strangle spreading the stain
Training the tantalizing soul past return or repent
As shaking hands fight back against a behemoth
Accepting the blood into his blazing wounds.

The table left splinters on his flesh
A beast bewitching his soul to create a crimson crusade
Cooled only by the frigid air and a swaying door
Crickets and frogs continue their lives
While he sits covered in bile
Puss and blood lines his rot
Jet black reaching his soul
Becoming darker than the starless night sky
Waving goodbye as their souls will never meet again
After the twine was split for a wall's fresh paint
Layers applied by hand for a grotesque display

A knightly knife embedded in an abomination
Abhorrent agonizing screeching amen
Another has risen to become foul
And the hunger drips through him
Only to be brought back to life
Craving crimson and crusading carnage
Nothing like the bitter champagne left over
Drunken from bloodied glasses
Shined before leaving for a cell
With tattered seats staining the mind
Driving away to hunger
Never will he make such a mistake again.

8

A missing man
Driven away into pitch black
Leaving a shadow behind
And stains along the elder couch
Not even turning the cushions would save me the sight.

Awakened by early day
A sizzle at noon
And a door swinging open on the sun's singing day
Back once more the pale man weeps
As if he was but a simple leaf
Dwindling through ages of wind and soot
Blanketed by a dark sheltered sky
Knocked down by the cruel fatigue of man
Being mortal is the cursed blessing still
No matter the mingled blood that lies under ruby eyes
Residing deeper than the bags of a restless soul
Truly there is no rest for the wicked
Feeling the eternal soul churning burn
Singing upon every thought and sought sight

By no means was the man an artist
Yet he wore his prideful paint from feet to face
Heading no blue warnings
Too slippery to be caught and the swiftest soot leaf
But does it matter when retribution comes knocking
The unapologetic scoundrel cackles in shady corners
Dealing in little pools of differing red
And the scarlet shades that haunt a new floor
Panels reborn as evidence for a dead man's crime
Blazing a silent trail that only lingers in mind and air
Wretched smelling sulfur creek along these halls
Walls smothered layer by layer
Trying to find his tomb of brimstone glory
And a throne befitting of a thrall.

9

Pitch black brought back
From vacancy to vacant seat
Stool by stool, day by day
A new layer of black to match another night
Spent breathing and cutting
Flesh and bones spiraling around a cramped room
All in a hushed whisper
Lingering through the starless sky
Painting a beautiful mural of crimson crowing gold
Craving a gilded meal without touching the rancid meat to
chapped lips
Reflecting upon the scarlet fluid that paints more and more
walls
With his heart set on a masterpiece.

Scrawling along the empty halls and sorrowful streets
Here lay five dead found drained on the beach
From basin to basin until a sudden splat
The artist moves forth with his haunting brush
Gigglishly smirking with each stroke
Letting it dance along each wall and streetlamp
Stretching the pools thin

Swirls of scarlet fury reminisce on the streets
Frowning upon the blackened corpse
Kept alive by rubies and soot
And another jet set suit worn down
Stained with the streets along with the newborn flesh
As laughter bounces off walls.

Finding home after death was easy
But feeling it was a wicked victory
And cruelties had shook
But never will he waver again
The thin and tough wood snapping on dry palms
Seeking the settling metallic scent
To silence the burning screams that linger
After all this time and still, he remains
Pitch black except to the core
Where it is blue no more.

10

Another night
The pale shadow is missing
Pitch mist dissipated along each vent
And peace returned to a silent house
Still shaken from the first night
Both I and the house remained in an awkward silence
As sitting in the eye of the storm is all too eerie
While each of the floorboard's creaks is a bit too bleak
Empty but full of dust and leftover soot
Smeared along sweaty palms and dry fingertips.

Every cough on the silent night startled the aging home
And the pale moonlight burning my flesh
Truly it was worth pursuing another purpose
To dance away another night
Sinking my teeth into a new pool of colorful curses
Grasping a new brush and the broken one left in ashes
A slippery swirl of grey across the scarlet breeze
Returning to the scene of an ancient crime
To clear out the land of the behemoth once more.

I was ill met by moonlight
When a knocking door was answered only with a pail
Floating in the crimson drink was speckled ashes and a
vial.
The vile smell told me that there was more
The scent trailed from corpse bushes
Oozing aromas were met with green spit
A chunky but loose fluid
Bits and pieces danced along the vile bile drifting in the
air
None showed a sign of dwindling when the sun rose to
burn it
Never again will these eyes see the same.

Spiraling in the pitch black haze
Decorating and throwing each morsel wildly
Rampantly raging through once silent streets
Now my pale face will be met with screams
And the tears of begging youth
Wishing for a savior or a loved one's life
While I paint the house family by family
Keeping the wretched screaming clinging to my own soul
As we all rot away together but die alone.

11

Truly there is no rest for the wicked
With a cursed tongue and bloodied hands
This shirt was once white
The suit was black some time ago
Now the red has stained, and the soot lingers
Ashes remain on his fingers
And when the steak knife falls on another screamer
Silence is once again achieved
Forgotten when the rubies find another
Painting a burning mural along each sheet
Every wall or road a canvas for the bestial urges.

Demonic hunger for blood
A lust like no other
Past the point of no return
Where the pitchforks seep poison
While fires lick the patrons
Participants in prevailing punishment
Much too cruel to be called justice.

Hunger hurts each and every day
And biting down on another's spirit fills me

Yet with each stomach full, it craves more
A town will fall tonight
With a duo of cursed hands
Raging moonlight in twin palms
Truly no rest for the wicked.

12

Clicking and clacking
I've seen the chains
A broadcasted tape to go through a lonely night
And a man once destined to be fried by a currently
forgotten chair
Dusty files resonate on my dry fingertips
While my cracked knuckles begin to bleed
White flesh with browning red revealing the chewy scarlet
beneath.
It is only now I worry if this flesh I own is cursed
Stained like a puppet smeared in the blood his master
dripped upon him
Staining the wood to become cherry
Invigorated by the splintery paint
Swirling with chunks in a reeking bucket.

Restless by the thought of a demon
Risen with the flesh of pale moonlight
Riding as a righteous reliance on pitch
Leaving behind his jet black marks and inky dots for me to
unearth
As I pick up precious pieces attempting to prevail

He has left and won't return unless to torment
Or perhaps groom an heir for the scarlet curse
To the drain, the precious liquid ruby from each star-
crossed blot in the shady blanket
Turning sheets to crimson and laughing at the night sky
Hiding from the sun like an immortal ashen worrywart
Yet rushing from building to building, gliding from town to
town
A storm of inky havoc upon those unlucky enough to find
him.

Harvesting is all I can do
For now, my strength will only fail me
As I look out the window and see him returning
Tattered and cold
Alone against the moon in the tattered black
Sleeves cut down to white
Then past it to moonlight skin
Bags beneath those glistening ruby eyes
Smiling contently as the wind brings him back
He returns to the shadow he left on the couch
And I lock the doors once more tonight.

13

Can the jet black repent
With rubies and scarlet gold
Being bleached and dried in the sun
For hopes of a soul saved?
The fire behind scarlet eyes says not
And the dark night skies flowing for the shaken dreamer
Pale and dancing with the moonlight
Sipping ale and such pleasantries waiting for the next
pitiful customer
In a bar of ailment and metallic booze
Drowning in the gilded stupor
Swaying hips along the breeze
Rusted blades with crusted red like human porcupines.

Panicking people in droves
As he waits to shoot them down like doves
Gracefully falling in a hazy rainy reddening fantasy
Chugging away sorrows in a corner store
Wine tasting went wrong with waters run red
A raging and ravishing sight for a sickened psycho
Or a lip-licking beast in moonlight's flesh
Tasting only the finest such a place has to offer

Stumbling over a scarlet sea and tripping on a soaking splintery mop
Falling together into the puddle
Laughing as the hallucination begins to fade and the headache sets in.

Rolling over and into a sting
As a door breaks down and bullets fly
To watch a partner's head get skewered by a broken handle
To then be twisted and contorted and thrown as a distraction
Watching the pale man's jaw unhinging as he huddles in laughter
Taking a bite of the stringy flesh
Laughing as cold steel meets the second man's head
Between the eyes a river forms
As he drops beside his headless companion
While dead set coddles a wounded shoulder
And pale moves towards the swaying moon once more.

14

Days.
Months.
Time is slipping from my hands.
My youth filled with flavorful exhaustion
Spiced up by labor trying to make ends meet
Struggling by all ends to put meat on the table
Overworked or hardly working
When the days are filled with looking elsewhere
Fingers furiously typing away
Searching for more with spiral notebooks of scribbles and
sprawlings
A pen dancing just to break under the pressure
Empty again and again
Leaving them in rows of crumpled paper caskets along the
floor
Manilla and white are blinding after so long.

The bland colors wear down at my eyes
And this shovel is killing my back
Where has my life slipped to
Research and occultism while suffering from tedious
trends and graphs

Perilous papers prevailing in sleepless nights of pity and
worth
Digging with dirty fingers that only continue to dry with
my hands
Becoming pale and flaking off the in warming breeze
When the skies tell us to toss our sleeves aside
And black goes out of fashion to become a death wish in
the making
Sweat raining down like the salty beads it has always been
Yet it's still not hot enough to match the burning inside of
my urn
Trying to uncover what needs to be done.

Each day has been slipping through my nimble fingers
And my limbs grow weary from stress and late nights
Waiting for the pale and scarlet curse to return
For another bucket to be stored
Brushes disappearing in thin air
And haunting murals to burn the streets eyes
Wickedly giggling as the moon rises
Laying like the dead when the sun's burning embrace rises
once more
It's only now I have one wish
For sleep to wash over me
And not be woken until the world's end.

15

Awoken by a cold breeze
Shards of glass to sweep skittishly
Looking behind me I see him asleep
Perfectly aligned to avoid the sun
And as the son, I seek answers
What is this man lying before me?
The sleepless nights won't whisper it to me
As I fall wistfully in sloppy blankets and sheets.

The sun, such a pleasant contraption
A contradiction to the life I now live
Proof at the week's end that holy stone can singe my flesh
Chunks of fitted wood polished to positively burn me on touch
With toxic water to wet fingers
Even I know the pitch black revival has brought me back weakened
Yet I remain stronger than the pitiful souls stolen from mere sock puppets
Yapping away until yesterday
Cold is my preferred warmth.

This glass hurts my hand
The sun cracks my head with a rusty shovel
Once used to bury a man
Now the relic is rusted with dirt-encrusted
It remembers as well as I
The death of a fallen man
And it too fears him as risen
Yet stained beyond repair
Tattered and torn like the soot layered suit
But as he turns and falls into the sun.

My mind burns as the beam hits me
I can feel my flesh consider bubbling
But truly this is mind over matter
I was tempered by unending flames
And licked by vile and bile designs
This blood is too thick to make a little son burn
Even with such disrespect
Leaving me here as lead drops from my shoulder
A sharp pain tells me my flesh has returned
And I rise with the grimy tattered blanket
Shuffling to the kitchen
All that night's work earned me a snack
Didn't it?

16

He is not as I thought
No creature of the night but definitely Lucifer born
Borne by blazes and ashen sins
Floating in the breeze
Cooking away the time I was going to spend alone
Looking further into files and cases
Books and grimoires of old
These dusty tomes demand my attention
Staring at me through the leather bound skin.

Pages and pages
Time drifts away
As an army of unfortunate paper cuts appears on my
fingers and palms
I am much too desperate
Too attached and invested
Digging myself deeper in the soot and ash
The fog that clogs my lungs
Liable to death by excruciating dust and damaging dreams
Waking to another dreadful dreary hazy swirl
Like the snow's dance along every frozen night
Leaving briefly then taking me by storm

Another night wasted
More questions than answers
While I dread the morning's curse
And I hear my own agonizing screams for the terrors
Horrors that lash at the lacerated mind that torments me
Daring my patience each day I am forced to wake
As the kitchen drawers call me
And steel seeks my flesh and blood.

The cackling of a morning's end is the worst part
And like the prey I hunt, my sleep becomes the day
The bags keep piling above my frowning grimace
Luckily I only bleed internally
And the scars hide from the naked eye
Of the people I have long since left
While working alongside them every day
As I rest my head among these pages
Locked away with a lamp that's too bright
The doorbell will ring again, but nobody will answer it.

17

The guest
Draped in black silk, and smiling with beads around his
neck
Clutching a bottle of exotic waters in his chubby hand
A rosy-cheeked lord worshiper of the rosary
Faith and hope lie in the beads and bottled sea
Frowns furrow and ferment into fear
Terror and tremors while trembling
Praying in a weeping heap
This house is a haunted hell
No possession has had such strength as if the demon lays
in a stale shadow
Returning every morning for a restful slumber
Rather than worrying about jobs and lumber
Cutting down the hawk's precious mice
As it and its spirit flee skywards.

The man left with dried rivers
Head down once again in a frown
Crossing himself to seal his soul
In a sole attempt to save himself from the stench of sin
Walking away, getting quicker each step

Never quite a run to hold on to faithless pride
Hiding his trembling legs beneath a black robe
Sweating away the beads he forgot in haste to leave
Marking me as the sinful occult
As if I had a say in such matters.

The water he dropped sizzled on contact
With the floors and walls
Each old gnarled furniture
And the dust seemed to repel the splashes
Looking into the private study he screamed
Truly I am a blackened son
Native to the tomes so much darker than pitch
Old spines call ages of curses
Reminding that crusades of crimson have been a constant
continuity
And the missing faces that haunted cartons
Were found with ripped stomachs
Three lines and livers missing
Acid pouring and membranes burning
Such unfortunate owners to have kept their deaths silent
Not suicide but no clear culprit
And each page tells another story
Will I become another?

18

A day has gone
To sweeping like a craving maid
The lusty hunger swarming my lungs
As each breath called for crunching bones
And now these surfaces are untrustable
But my stain has sneakily spread
Like a spider's silky sickly web
Stuck along every edge and fiber of this home
Even old tomes I am not to touch.

One day out to set things ablaze
Flames to lick the summer sun
A nearby town now nearby ash
All from a simple hazy crash
Leading to bashing and breaking of bone
Salting the now white and gray road
With all steel to hone
Polish and puncture through veins
A kitchen's form of acupuncture
Butchering blazing heaps like fire
Spreading wildly through watery weather
As acid accents and pours from the gray cloudy sky

Rolling in like the rain with a poisonous pain
Dropping the match and lighting the cigar
The final ember and smoke of a town
Soot leaving lungs for lavish blackening skies
The only ember on a stick of once green.

Walking away with clapping hands
Wiping with a rag so easily disposed
Yet more valuable than the people that stood
But the craving was quenched and set away
Only to call to me like a chocolate cake
Screaming at me from the fridge or freezer
Too weak am I to not dig in
As sliver of hunger leads to a slippery slope of stolen
scarlet
One more night, just one more night
To gain the spoils I have won
And maybe then I can say this is all done.

19

One more night
Is all I can say
To avoid my own cold clammy embrace
Swaying with a dancing moon at night
And rooting further into my old home
Where I fear the old hidden texts
Long thought dead and buried
Now bathing under familiar lamplight
Maybe we have something in common after all.

Roots are found in the worst places
Digging under homes and snaking around riverbeds
Scaly bark burns with such ease
As does this midnight flesh
Pale and cold with the moonlight
But heating with the seasons
Or so it was rumored.

The internal cold never leaves
Emptiness and hunger drives me forward
Growling with my stomach and harvesting scarlet milk
Leaving it to crust in rusty metal

Scents colliding in the intoxicating steel
Paint for the streets
A mural for we
Who fear each new night and breath–
For the pale man's smile means only one horrible truth
The guillotine is back in town
Awaiting the villagers to quench its thirst
And nobody can stop this wicked contraption
Stomping through the scarlet starless street
Warmed only externally by the summer's cruel heat
Embracing the crescent moon
Me and my tipped buckets and brushes
Tanning in the bitter moonlight.

20

The moon has risen once more
For that reason, I cower in this dust veiled library
Page by page
Crawling hour by hour
Scrawling through notebook after notebook
Piles of pilfered papers
Thumbing through truth, lies, and loosened fact
Burning retinas upon a blazing mind
Racing from the whitened brown lake
Being poured each hour and warmed with milk.

Another night
Breathing and alive
Setting a trail ablaze
And a legacy to never be forgotten
These streets will be painted
By each painstaking hour, my work grows larger
Truly I will never be done
Until death do us part, as I once said
But now I know the errors of my past
Driven further than death's pool of madness and pitch
black dreams

To floating along each night sky
Seeing pearly gates and bracing for impact
The clouds will know flame as I fly.

Candlelight with a waxy dancing flame
A wick as pitch as his soul
And yet I remain here
A single ember among ashen corpses
Fingering through the numbing text
Awakening demons that shouldn't have been
And each night I waste on study
He burns down a thousand more
Yet I can feel a new presence
And its hot breath scalds my neck
Truly I have made a massive mistake.

As the sun rises my son descends
To the point where even he has left the home
Three nights ago, and I ponder his return
But I am a simple starving artist
Seeking to burn and churn the scarlet and crimson mesh
But the knocking on the door tells me of his return
Carrying much more bags than books
Black under exhausted eyes
Leaving me to get back to rest
In the shadow sitting silently on the couch
Another hard night's work for the both of us I see
Oh, what fools we truly are.

21

The house smells
Of another shadow stalker like me
And the ashes smell of inferno
Yet the shade around my son has grown
And horns tend to grow from the hunched inky figure that
follows him
That scent follows him and stains the room of horrid pages
It was part of the dusty papers
Burning the book did so little
He has found his host to haunt until they both go insane
Spiraling around the inferno – like lover's quarreling
Making a racket on the roads and riverbeds
Just two smiling corpses
Soot skin and missing eyes
Gouged out by the crows and vultures
Hungry for sight and recent knowledge
Truly the most matured scholars.

To the hospital we go
Avoiding kicking and screaming by dragging the two
scamps forth
Over my shoulder and down the road

Skipping to an old feeble man
Black robes and balding scalp
Scalding young passersby as eggs are thrown
And the chapels skeleton was wooden
Leaving the bricks under something so much weaker
Sitting down and waking my son up
With my ruby eyes unnerving the priest
Sitting behind a desk and gasping
For how could two territorial parasites
Not be clawing at each other
For rights of a hopeless host?

He was right about one thing
Through that whole time-wasting meeting
I am indeed a territorial man
And yet wrong about him being unremovable
For all of us can be removed
With the right equipment
I will not be messed with
By some pussyfooting preacher
Wishing for some money in a failing building
So, as we left and were gifted the burning water in five
large vials
I set out on a new nighttime endeavor.

22

The smell of gasoline
That sweet car's brew
In color but not in scent
Sloshing forth from a plastic spout
The cheap and dented red container
Never again will this man scam me
For once the wooden skeleton is burned
And he is desperately clinging to life
The building he devoted his life to will weigh him down
Into the depths of the abyssal void
Calling for his cheap soul.

The hole in his chest
Makes the screams almost too pleasant
As he drowns in crimson contaminated fuel
The stench was truly the most unpleasant part of the day
And while the proximity of crosses and water
That graced my moonlit flesh
To burn me in a once holy flame
My skin's new scars only set me forward
Dead set on drawing the perimeter
Keg after keg with sprinkled gunpowder

Wires and ticking from clocks and what not
All a symphony directed by the scarlet screams
Sloshing killed the silence of the night
A cruel and starless void that will always call for me
And in the twilight hours, I dropped the match on the liquid trail.

The fourth of July was a sweet one
Works of flame as my latest artform
Arson supplied by arsenic
The flames crackled along with me
Licking every bloodied blade
Green turned to grey and the chapel crumbled
And the moon smiled over me
Once the screams had stopped
And the flames died with our wicked laughter
I could rest easy with the moon once more
Fading with the pitch of the sky
To slumber another day away
Truly I have outdone myself.

23

Back to the dreadful and dusty pages
Days drowsily drained and time long lost
And now with an accomplice
Whispering secrets and lies into my ears
Never letting me lay in bed for too long
Poking and prodding at my flesh
My shadow haunts every step
Growling when I dare to eat
Trying to drive me into infernal torment
Until I collapse alone and afraid
Day after day.

It's sickened horned men like these
The con artist
Trying to swipe a soul and burn the evidence
Just for the pleasure of getting away with it
To cackle as it's foolish host rots
Bleeding on the floor again
But this time the bandages have dissipated
And nothing can staunch the deepening flow
As the hanging rope lowers
And both hands collide

Combining for one last effort
To rise and fall
Levitating in the air like a corpse on the breeze
Stinking up the sorrowful forest.

I find a home in the dead trees
Pale pages poison me at each touch
Labyrinths of inky blots tricking the eyes
Truly no space left for the divines
Stalking each page with a pen and book of my own
Notes flushed and lacerated
Crumpled around the floor in netted baskets
Sparse space left between cheap plastic
Too little time left to toss
And perhaps mistaken pages remain
One that many hold the key
And maybe even one that could save me.

24

Every day his putrid scent permeates the house
And I slouch on the couch
What is a father to do–
When a son turns into two?
And one is rancid like burning flesh
A mere shadow of wicked dealings
I will have to strike him down
My son is my flesh and blood after all
The house is still mine
And I have no intentions on returning to that solemn grave
At the very least not alone.

The sun rose on a cloudy day
And many rest easy
While the moonlight dances on my flesh
Given strength by the stars and the crescent sphere
Curved and sharp like a farmer's blade
Sickly hanging in the sky
Cloaked like a small carver in a pocket
Waiting to be thrust into the sweet rusting red
The metallic wine just dying to drop
Letting everything burn up to crispy crumbs

I must forsake my cursed blood

Even if only for a night

And a cheap store run

Leaving slashes and gashes along streets like open sores

As the rain pours, it triggers the scent of ashy flesh and pus

Seeping through walls and infecting the nearest wounds

One more night, and it will be ready

I will take my territory

Be it by trigger or blade

Tooth or nail

Or perhaps a devious contraption of toxic rain

The blessed water in vials

Into the skin and through the veins

Trapping the shady fireflies in a jar

All I need is a bit of rope

And perhaps the burning book

As even if my singed flesh never recovers

I will stake out my territory

I will claim the lifeblood that's rightfully my own.

25

The news talks about three more burnings
And ruined Sunday mornings for the masses
Or those just sitting in classes
To hear that blood burns and trees lost branches upon
branches
No traces but the bitter gasoline
Except for the Son, who sits strapped
Fearful of the needles in his veins
Open eyes that could never fully display the horror.

The jars were ready, spoke the chilled Father
Flicking needles and filling them
Rubber gloves saving his hands from the acid
As tubes pump and spiral
Draining the basins and watching the spiraling madness
Watching the shaking screamer shudder
A mouth forcefully closed to avoid a headache
Of an unwilling boy at the doctors
Much too fearful of the sharp contraptions.

Water pumping from blessed containers
In the most unholy experiment subjected upon a Son

The screams don't come from his whimpering whispers
They come from the growing and shaking shadow
Runes etched in every inch of the wall and floor
A circle of five points and the star once sought by devilish
crusaders
Even the chair feels the horror vibrating through it
Screeches scar the poor Son
Salty rivers stain a face contorted in agony
And the etchings on his arms begin to bleed
Arching back and staring at the ceiling
His back and shoulders being torn by shady claws
Burning rivers of agonizing sorrow and screams permeate
the cluttered room.

The room shakes with his giggling
And Father paces while the water drains
An ancient pot on a pedestal awaits the shade
Placed in a heavy box and set down the river
To drown in sorrows while breathing dull air
Stale and cracked while leaving scars
And once more this territory is mine
The burns are but an insignificant sacrifice
To be rested off like the new wounds.

It is here that we see
A madman's exorcism
And a boy wounded and wound in bandages
Medicated wraps can do only so much
For the whispers and screams have taken their toll
If a deal were to be stuck
Just giving away a worthless soul

So many could have been saved but no
'Twas the fear of dying that keeps him weary
And the sleepless months that bore into him
He was once again alone in this, and truly it was for the
better
Yet as the marks still stain the library
And pages soaked with watered down blood
One relic does remain
A single silver bullet
Wasting away in a wine glass
Taking a soak in holy water
The last case scenario was forgotten by a tired Father
And stashed away for another day.

26

With just a simple deal
So much could have been avoided
How lousy was I that I wouldn't listen
He said, "Just listen here to me child
You've burnt too many candles on both ends
Each more bitter than the last
So, shake my hand
A mere soul away from saving thousands
From a man of the pitch-black night."

Days and nights keep me astute
More wicks crumbled at my tired touch
And it was her who said "Goodbye
I once thought we were close
But ever since you left I know that any love
Or what was thought
Was just a lie."

Now I lay here alone
Spinning on what they all said
Straining my ears while I stain my eyes
Burning them away from the inside

Widened by the caffeinated brews
Vomiting while wired and passing out again
On these ruined notes I will sleep another night
Just to wash it off in the morning
But the one thing that I can never scrub off
is the people I've lost
To the pitch black flame and by my own hands
Scrawling and clutching on pages and harsh leather
I miss the dead and the absent
Both absent forevermore
As I search evermore for the end
Be it in old pages
Or even in something as simple as a wet bullet.

27

Freedom by fire
Body separated from screaming soul
Re-defining revolution read in red runic etchings along the
street
A refined rebirth rebuilt in moonlight
And I'm just here to watch the flames
Reminding me of a home I wish to forget
On the crimson rows of nighttime fences
A gate of sharpened tips
Where manners stalk the fine wine and laughter
And over extravagance reigns supreme.

The spoiled wanderers of wealth and smiles
And I find with them a sense of familiarity
Between the swaying and towering gowns
All in spiraling circles
Hand in hand it reminds me of one
Whom I almost forgot among scarlet and flame
Maybe they will meet my moonlit hand tonight
But for now, I watch and wish to join them
Even if just for a night before the flames
To watch the wonderment of spirits and specters

But truly it's tonight where something must be done
As these busy people leave each day
On a hunt for something much or delectable
Then what's rotten here on the table.

It's in these dancing drinks
That I find a dash of solace
As the moon descends on the manor
My manners firmly leave
Crashing a party is one thing
But setting the dance floor on fire is another
Watching the faces shift
The cheap scent of the gas station stains their colognes and
perfumes
A bitter breath ending in ashes
Swirling from the newly opened ceiled
Crushed by the rubble and still set ablaze
All of them have taken their maiden voyage to sharper
gates
If they thought these flames were harsh
They don't even know a quarter of it.

28

Life is like a vengeful razor
It cuts so much more than once
But it's necessary to keep clean
Or just lacerate flesh deemed deserving of sweet death
But I and life are akin
As my hands remain stained
We have cut more than once
Much more than enough
To satisfy a bestial urge
The craving to feel
Something physical to distract from the abstract
Dabbing another cheap paper towel on the crimson rows
Giving way to a soaking scarlet crop
To harvest then toss away
Hiding the shame from the same world
That forced my hand in the first place.

I wish I had truly gone numb
So I would feel no guilt
So the vase's words of vices would be meaningless
So I could lose myself and flee from the dusty pages that
haunt me

He hasn't left quite yet
The conman waits in his tomb
Whispering his last words before being locked in the
rusted steel
Chains envelop the heavy box
As the pale man tosses it into a trunk
His voice hushes for the last time
Driving far away for disposal
And drowning him in a stream
Watching the box sink and lose its final breath
A bubble pops on the surface
And we watch in silence.

Homeward bound yet wishing it would burn next
To wipe away each excruciating night
All that would remain is ash along the breeze
Oh, how I long for that
Solace in a lonely fate
And peace in his absence
It devours me as I lay and rest
Slowly healing from the rivers raked behind me
Each minute gets longer
As I wish for it all to end in only the most befitting tragedy.

29

As my son rests in the car
My delightfully weakened unwilling host
Yet he is my guest as he drifts asleep
And I lock the car doors
Walking forward into the night sky
I want to feel the warmth of a light flame
Making crimson and flesh a crispy mixture
I am truly just a caged animal
Sinking my teeth into the next meal
And I tend to like my meat past well done
For only the scent of fresh screaming steak.

In all honesty
I purchased these fine cheap wares
And the only way to check quality is use
So tonight, I will set up the grill
For a nighttime snack
I'm just here pouring out the gas
On a sleepily silent cabin
A family of three sleep in their warm little beds
Only to wake to each other's screams
And the sweet scent of gas

I thank that empty station every visit
The undiscovered corpse behind broken glass
Stowed away on a road's offshoot
Without lights, it's easy to miss among the trees
Although the pumps are running empty
And all the food is rotten
It's quite a fine place for the essentials
Of this little game, I love to play.

I walked back to the car
After a nice long smoke came to a close
And the smoke stained the air
To a Son still resting
And a stomach ferociously growling
I think it's time to eat a nice meal
Before heading home
And doing it all again when the moon calls my name.

30

The Ember and the Ash
Father and Son
Driving on a steady road
They spoke in hushed murmurs
As if they lost their words like strays
Staying in a run-down diner
Eating a meal while staring to the outside
The window was dusty and marked with snot
From the lady who sat there previously
With a loud and obnoxious mutt.

Ashes are found after flame
The once beloved child of what will soon die
To be revived and come back to the grey specks
Swirling in the midsummer breeze like dandelion puffs
among the trees
Hoping to flee from the fire's tongue
Licking all the fools that come near it.

Flame is found by an inspired strike
Rising from the dead
Eating away the ground it sways on

A bloody crusader on his newfound conquest
Scarlet loves to dance with orange and yellow
Deepening the warming colors that flicker
The reason behind the burnt wicks
And cuts along the pages.

It is here that we all watch
The ditch be dug further
A gap of a gash that only grows darker
While the stormy clouds brood and brew in the sky
It's now that the only question is time
At this point the reason why is clear
And that bullet soaking is the key
But the boy is too squeamish to fire a gun
And his Father remains proud of it
For what good is a violent host
When the parasite wants to dig deeper
Finding its home in a fleshy puppet
Miserably turning another page
As agony begins to mutate
And animalistic rage begins to boil.

31

Reading these books in bed
With itchy bandages of irate proportion
Goes together like water and glue
It's like a railroad heading straight for you
The infernal void that prods me awake at night
But now at least it has no voice
And my shadow remains hornless
Ever since the conman was dunked in the river
These wounds have begun a grueling heal
Cruel agonizing stress keeps me awake
As I cut on these dusty pages
My red stains the wrapping
Like a bleeding mummy being laid to rest
While his eyes are open to the scalding sun.

Could the burnt out hole of flames
Truly be as horrid as this
With each waking moment, I bleed
My silenced screams keep me awake every night
And these pages never help
Decoding etchings and runes
Scribbling away to solve every mystery

Signs and symbols haunt my mind
Illustrations from the fiery depths
Words that only get worse and worse
The sound of the dead and dying
Like cold waves on a rough beach
Blackened by the filthy grime
Compiled over years of malnutrition
Leaving scaled bags to limply float
And I wish to sleep alongside them.

Every night I'm cursed with the moon
And like a screeching bird
The sun tells me to slap myself together
Work calls and I must drag myself back to life
Just to squander it later in the night
Delving further into the pungent pages
"How much is enough?"
I would have said if I had not lived it
But now I call upon flames
To save me from myself.

32

I am cured by the moon
It heals my flesh once again
As I bring the hammer down
The crunch is so pleasant in the stinging air
Snapping skeletal necessities
Smashing it into a fine dust
The beats get lighter and lighter
As the meat is tenderized
And any backbone mixes with the pulp
The beautiful sound of a final breath
Gasping greedily for air that will never come
Lungs too compressed to embrace the warm winds.

It's here beside the blue faces
With makeshift smiles held up by popsicle sticks
That I watch the corpses sway
Strewn about and hug on trees
Inners became outers in the pale moonlight
Bathed in the pitch black blanket of a soot-filled sky
Smoke rolling with the clouds
And flames cackling on the breeze
Dancing with their precious children

The ashes that grow as everything decays
Dwindling on the breeze like the dead
With a futile final wish to be spread on the sea
Grey spectacles dancing on the breeze
That final teary goodbye.

It's here that the draining is done
On this old farm's overgrowth
Hanging here is the beef
Dripping the deepening crimson into buckets
Each night the buckets are filled again
And the basin sustains my burnings
By blood, I can cast away any semblance of mortality
Cured by the night's lovely gift
Unhinging my jaw to take the basin's contents
And within me, I have a week's supply
The basin trickles down to the pale man
Quenching the thirst of fifteen years of flame.

33

A silent night is met by cackling flame
The businessman was on another trip
Out to dinner, I assume
As he loves his meat both freshened and raw
A direct source of chunky crimson laced flesh
I took a page from his book
And toted tomes to the center of a field
Stacking the dusty papers and chicken scratch
Gently and carefully constructing a tower
One by one the notes became the triangular roofing
Topped by the list of the dead I once loved
The black ink stared longingly into the night sky's eyes
Sparkling with a dim but newfound hope
Stars like children hanging alone
Swayed by the light breeze dying alongside them
Delicately dangling in a dreadful waste.

At first, it was a circle
Then I got sloppy
Sloshing it out of the cheap plastic
The putrid scent filled my nostrils and the pungent pages
And I struck a single match

It danced almost unwillingly in the horrors of the dark
Flinching but of its own accord
Brave like an unsteady man of unflinching might
It wasn't very bright but it was about to make prevalent
light
A pyramid of flames erupted
Darkened by the hushed secrets
And for a moment nothing burned
As if asking me if this is what I really wanted
But as I drove away I looked back at the bright that dared
to pierce the night
A strong blaze to cure my blight
Although I do fear we'll be together once more
As pitiful residents of ash.

34

A liquor store on a lonely street
Shady dealings under the table
Knock thrice and entry is a guarantee
Welcome to this speakeasy
Rebuilt and repurposed after the recession
Giving some a digression from the depraved depression
Haunting them until this room
Where anything goes.

First, the dogs come in
Then the sweet bagged sugar
Powdered as always
Standing next to the crystals
While money is thrown haphazardly
And the pipes and needles meet
The most genuine of maniacal laughter can be heard
Wasting nights away through the soot-like smoke
Clogging each and every dirty breath
As if they are all nothing but kitchen sinks
Drowned by hairballs from a dying cat
Turned over on the counter and spitting vile bile
Unable to even produce vomit from its stomach

Starved and depraved, defiled by the world
While the light fades from its starless eyes
Like a man who has lost his home
Living in a cardboard box and wasting away
Accompanied only by moonlight and rags.

The poison was just fine
But a pleasure for only mortality's outcast
Morality tossed aside for just one more night
As the barking gets louder and louder
The knife carves through another neck like butter
A cheap and choppy blade that does the job just right
Crusted with blood and rust to season each diced meat
A fresh meal for the hounds
Starless eyes containing pillars of flame
Truly we three get along the finest
While chomping away and laughing on the grimy ground
Littered with corpses that lost their heads
They flew too high
Like Icarus, they needed to be struck
And as the fire, I reserve the rights to each slippery soul.

35

Finally, a night of peace
And the howling soon subsided
Two lovely scrappy little mutts just don't stop singing
Looking for a little attention
An oddity to be brought home
As the pale man sleeps
They wrap around his legs
And like loyal servants' growl when prodded
But truly they are very docile
Nature overriding nurture I suppose
But then again I don't know their original home.

They followed me as if I was a trail
Spiraling through Oregon with high hopes and full
stomachs
Little did they know I'm the organ trail
And I have no connection to the state's fine doctors
Nor the markets that eats pups like these
Shoving the living in oversized crockpots
Watching the slow grueling deaths
Of red rooms and darker markets
An amoral stain that gives grotesque goods

Yet its mere existence shows the beauty of man
The smuggling, lying, cheating
All for smile and wealth
But so meaningless in death and to me.

My room is mine once more
I can lay in fresh sheets
A warm hug from fleecy wonders
Drowsily waiting for the night to wash over me
As now it seems to dash to the day
Restfully lulling and for the better
My problems burnt with those books
Buried within fragmented memories as the pale man once was
The moon no longer burns my flesh
And the nights I dare to stay awake are my own
Stumbling around the town in a delicate daze
Melting by the warm oranges and yellows on a displaced sky
Blurrily blending on a soundless spherical stone
Taking life much less responsible.

Some nights while I rest or return he leaves
Occasionally coming back at the same time
Cheap whiskey stains his breath and his smile
Burping and stumbling in a spiraling stupor
Like I once did in those crazy youthful parties
It brings me back to the days I first met her
Reminding me of the cruel hand fate gifted her
The first blood that stained my soul
Only truly tainted in the infernal depths

As the blood seeped into my veins and my eyes opened
I became jet set with twin rubies
Leaving for this bitter world
Laughing at its endless inky void
Reviling in screams while I live out this dream
Just five more minutes until work
One more night
Just one more night.

36

My sparkling rubies brought me here
To the sampling of crimson liquors
A taste too divine it brings a hellish punishment
And I say a prayer for the wicked
Since we never rest
Making scarlet wine
Whining in a stream of tears
Flames lick us all in the wasteland
The black field that's darker than night
The luckiest of us all is the scarecrow
Hands nailed into a splintery post
Head dangling without the strength of a neck.

Loose flesh is swinging in the breeze
Like beef in a butcher's freezer
Waiting to be carved into a fine meal or two
Wasting the most important parts
Tossing them down and away
Even if it's frozen eyes would open
Its body wouldn't function
And it's now that I leave the house
Done with the bitter memories

Like acid on an open wound
They sizzle and stretch each gaping hole
Red pools becoming scarlet lakes
I can see each and every tainted face screaming
And I seek to add more
To save me from the torment
Or at least grasp wicked retribution
I will not go back alone
But I will strike at the pearly gates
They have eluded me too long
Taken away too much
I miss her but what I truly miss the most
The ability to feel and breathe.

Every night I run and feel alive
All I can feel is adrenaline and dread
I much prefer the feeling of blood running down my face
It's much too easy to get drunk on tears
Dwindling away with each starting flame
It's only me that remains
I crawled out for a reason
Sweet, sweet revenge found in a black sky
One more night
And maybe I will go over the hill
Overdosing on hyper swirls and spirals of scarlet joy
I'm bound to find that cloudy place
To tear down those gaudy gates
One more night and I will find it
Divines will strike me down

And I'll rise again
Just one more night
To stop climbing
And start soaring.

37

I have returned once more
To a house claimed from the divine that closed the gates
Taking her and leaving me
Letting me fall through the crust to the core
Where pitchforks and infernal truths poison ears
Back to the ashes of a preacher's demise
It was all worth it
Perhaps the stairway I seek is here
Or it fell with the rest of the rubble
It's all settled and painted now
The laughter of young rascals just waste around here.

Homeless sleeping among broken bricks
A sort of solace resides here
As if hopes and dreams died
It's all waiting to be rebuilt
I'll have to fix that soon enough
But today I think I'll stand with the rats
Looking into the stormy sky
The rain feels smooth on my moonlit flesh

These stained faces rest easy
As if they don't know of the wolf among them
Little sleeping sheep with tattered wool
Swaying in the light breeze like little white saplings
I think tonight I'll eat out
I heard of a place downtown
With powder lined on tables
Booze bubbling and spilling all around
A cozy little den that I would love to boil
Watch the faces melt from ecstasy to agony
I miss her from day to day
But I hide it in crimson
That craving is so much worse than her absence
I feed both like a cursed blaze
On my trail, I lie and wait
Perhaps I'll skip dinner but not breakfast
Proving that I can handle the sun's embrace
To the Son, that is resting like a newborn.

38

I shouldn't have gotten too comfortable
The blues caught up with me once more
Lead wizzes through the air
Like cheap plastic in a park
Or bleached skin just waiting to hit something
Perhaps the crying child or the shaking wife
When vehicles turn to weaponry
Like an old-fashioned hummer
Stolen from some old garage
The blood of the mechanic stains the front
If only that made this gaudy yellow turn orange
A trail of tar will lead them to me
But I wouldn't mind a nice meal.

Passing through glass windows
Towers and mannequins staring
With nowhere else to be who wouldn't
Besides the nighttime shoppers and raging drunks
Three sat vomiting into a sewer grate
Until that great splatter of their soft tissues broke against
my car
Leaving trails of mucus like a sick child

Or a snail rushing to its humble abode
One foot, now two
Then three then four
Slithering away through the streets
A fork on the cracked road like a cracked tongue
As rain begins to fall on this dreamily dreary night
It all falls like tears
Gunshots clog my ears
I'll make sure they hear each other scream
Squealing on my plate
It's just a game of cat and mouse
With a dash of role reversal
A failure like they have never seen.

I roam where the alley cats call home
And wait in the shadow
Phasing into the inky void awaiting footsteps
Both of their backs turned like fools
These two children ran into the haunted house unattended
But I'll give them something to remember
Carving into their oh so precious flesh
Drenched in their lifeblood they once held dear
They fall next to one another and say goodbye
Except all I hear is their screams
Dinner is served
And it's time I went to the barbeque
With forks and knives in hand.

39

He is out with the hounds
The third head on a hellish beast
To hell with them and their expensive taste
I'd much rather a T-bone than a filet mignon
But he never uses money that's his
The pale man is living jet set off other's funds
Digging through dens and pits
He won't be sent on his maiden voyage into the depths
But perhaps he will be sent deep enough to never come
back
That's not my problem or job anymore
I quit, I'm done
I'd rather shoot myself with a cackling rusty gun
Deepen the lakes hidden on my hushed arms
For now, it's the bittersweet taste of rum
The ABC's are alcohol, blurs, and crimson
The trifecta of my new life
Night or day it's just a haze
And I much prefer it that way.

It's nights like these that call to me
Watching the fall trees die in wait

Shouting at a familiar shadow for another
Shot after shot like a scarlet gunfight
Just like the one downtown
With witnesses reporting man fading into the pale
moonlight
A wicked grin graces his face
Pictures and photos
Recordings and audio
All of them haunting but not from a sloppy hubris
He wants people to see his face
See the man of lead torches
Blazing a bloody trail of horrific beautiful madness
Artfully painting the world from his inky black canvas
Glory and honor found in the scarlet screams of stolen
souls
Set for a tormented tortuous existence
And although I have my fleshy exterior
We have the same fear and hell
A gift from the pale man that stalks every night
Much more ferocious than the last
His venomous fangs seep into more flesh
Blind purposely to the innocence and youth of victims
Creating a scarred generation of imperfections and
quaking nighttime terrors.

It is simply sickening
My everlasting habit of worry
I await the numbness of a blurred world
As it all bubbles up
Spilling out like the contents of a boiling pot

A raw chunky stew stains the ground of this all but empty bar
I won't be able to crawl back into that car
It looks like this calls for another night on the floor
Next to the corn and chunks of undigested meat
Floating in its rich and thick pool
While the light fades from my sight
And a man comes walking with a mop we are both too familiar with
I see that look of disappointment and shame
The kind that a familiar stranger would have
The look of an old but forgotten friend
Is the last thing I see before the pitch black sweeps over me
And I'm swept into the cold of another dream.

40

I was not driven to my home
And yet this house feels more comfortable than mine
Funny how almost being raised by a friend's family makes
them yours
I do miss his parents
Dying just last month to a horrible car crash
Luckily it was a mere accident
It's been rough on him
Yet he doesn't descend
He has always been that straight edged boy I grew up with
Laced in a melancholy light and breathing it both in and
out.

Nobody understands the freedom of another night
One more just to live and breathe
Each bloody breath and decadent step brings me closer to
home
Yet this time far from the shackles
But I have to ask if they were truly that terrible
As a weapon, they weren't
Guiding me to those precious rubies
Gouged from bloody eyes

Choked out by cold steel links
I can still hear his pleas for another breath
Meanwhile, I snapped one of his sharp horns
Bringing the stake through his spine and out his chest
Leaving nothing but a pile of dismembered flesh
And a tattered heart on a cracked bone.

Given fresh clothes and a single direction
I remember many late nights on this couch
The cracks along the leather call me home
But is it home if I'm awake?
My only full escape is restless sleep
Even when the sun begins piercing the sky
I gain my warmth from the blanket
Crashing like a misguided plane
Drowning in my own restless dreams
The seas call my name again
As usual, I'm happy to oblige.

Today I don't think I should stop
I'm on another excursion
Farther into the heart of the city
In its center lies hope
For the young and the old
Hospital's bridged by glass
Where treatment and research is funded and founded
Trying to solve the unsolvable
A mortality that eats much too quick for their liking

I say it's time for a bit of survival among the fittest
These cattle will meet an early end
I am hungry after all
And I'll happily cater a selfish buffet.

41

It's that dream again
Not the one with my teeth falling out
Or falling just to gracefully splat against a taxi
The one where everyone dies around me
My shackles are a never-ending void
Where nothing but me exists
Every person I have ever cared for
The people I love the most
All torn away by some wicked entity
That travels by moonlight with a wicked grin
While I am no fool
And know who this bestial crusader is
It's shameful for me to admit
I've woke up screaming at least three times
Just to be comforted by an unrelated brother
Lulled to sleep like a mummified child
Petrified and wrapped in white wool
The only calming warmth I have met in a while.

It's here that I let it all out
And through the blanket's new tear stains
Whaling like a blubbering buffoon

Every vomit induced nightmare
The restless nights
Blood and scars all dried
The lies to keep everyone from it
I told him everything
Even about the pale man and the vase
Now lost in a downtown river
To be unearthed one day by an unlucky soul
Sadly, we discovered who that star-crossed and cursed
individual was
And now I miss her like any lover would
It's the feeling of a knife being pounded through my chest
Like a slow needle sewing a fresh scarlet rage into me
To bless my future steps
Washing my face in the kitchen sink
Breathing a shallow breath
Too much has been taken from my grasp.

It looks like the con man got a murder under his belt
Through hushed whispers, he dragged her to infernal
damnation
He gave her what I was too scared to take
If only I took that deal while it stood
It wouldn't have backfired so
The pale man would be in his rightful ashen throne
She would be alive
And I would have saved the lives of so many
Stopped scarring from spreading like wildfire
I not only selfishly denied the con artist
But greedily I revealed each and every bit of information
The months of late nights finally took me down

The sea washed over me again
But this time I had a crewmate on this rickety shoddy
canoe
Sailing towards an unsteady mooring
Be it dawn or dusk.

42

Each night is a gift
And like a child on Christmas, I lust over opening it
Tearing into a fresh corpse
Disposing of the bitter chunks in the newfound cavity
With cold steel as by brush
And lead to back every stroke
I will carve my name into the history books
Or at the very least the nightmares of a generation
In doing so I promise I will not disappoint
My only purpose is the customer's happiness
Found simply by a decapitation
Suddenly I have a fresh face served on a silver platter.

Twin rubies always scare the city's cattle
Once the night takes them
As the white dissipates I feel the inky black down to my
fingertips
And just like wicks, I will light each simpleton's skull
Simply this city is just an urban jungle
And as the farmhand, I reserve a right
To sample the beef firsthand
Drinking the cursed crimson milk

Staining another bitter breath
Making it all the more sweet
Fresh ambrosia at its finest
A decadent delicacy that sends shivers along the tongue
Such a taboo practice in a terrible excuse for a farm
And I reserve the right to each dime of profit
Or at the very least each morsel and drop.

I stand alone in this cold and cruel moonlight
A palm extended towards the sky's sickle
Covered in staining scarlet sinful lust
That ravenous bestial hunger
Dripping from my fingertips is the essence of not just one
family
They will fuel these broken wings
I will ascend to glorious retribution and reign the hell that
was forced upon me
That pearly throne will be mine
But for now, I pick these bones clean
The ribs really were worth the money.

43

It's nights like these I stop to think
Where is the pale man tonight?
I know the moonlight calls his cursed name
Wanting its fair share of crimson
His policy of one more night is truly a scarring
misdemeanor
The note he left states only horrid intentions
To burn down a hospital for children and sickly victims
Sickening is the only word that comes to mind
I wish my hands had the strength to do
Anything to resist his wishes I wish these legs had a dash
of energy
And for another night I hide with my old friend
This place has been my temporary home
We both need a shoulder to cry on
Another day wasted in a haze
A goodbye then skipping off to work
And as I return home I don't need a bucket
No more browning pools of chunky green
Of which I needn't see much more

Upon returning home I see the hounds in slumber
Oddly tame except on the nights where flesh hangs from
their jaws
Their toothbrushes are permanently stained scarlet
These hornless bulls dream in a docile state
I can only hope their short hair stays decently groomed
Or else I have to chase them around with a brush
The scrubbing is all too much
But it's worth it to see them reformed
Although the nights where they disappear with him
I fear for them more than myself
With a declining health and a fire to their pitch black eyes
And patches of permanent crimson and night sky
I know they will not live much longer
And yet they will sleep on this couch
At least until the pale man meets a pearly end
Once more that bullet comes to mind
I must hide it from him
Before he becomes privy to the only object that gives me
hope.

A swift run to my second home
Hiding the glass in a box
Stashed under some clothes in the closet
It sits there awaiting use
I can only pray that the slow rusting makes no difference
Yet I doubt its real use
Going home I fear for the night
And turn on the news for a terrifying truth.

44

A man on his prevalent crusade
He stalks streets with hands jammed in tattered pockets
The blood dripping isn't only his victim's
The pale man looks up at the helicopter's camera
Smiling as it goes off course
As if the night erected a tendril and tossed it into the flames
The bellowing blazes take the streets
Houses and families
Businesses and employees
All meeting the same sorrowful end
The screeching will die with the flames
But for now, the night is warmed by the orange and red
Drunk off of its newfound infernal heat
Dead set on a single purpose
His rubies lost in the night of his starless eyes
And yet he has exceeding control of himself and the surroundings
Even as dark grey mist rolls in
Matching the darker sky
The rain is almost hesitant
Fearful of the death's cruel flame

Steadily moving forward
Even when the day crawls in
The clouds besmirch the sun's awakening light
Life won't go on here
He made sure of that
As the ashes were picked up by the breeze
It would take years for it all to dissipate
A minuscule moving volcanic hell is heading towards his
throne
Showing he is after a castle of glass
This conquest would not soon be forgotten
It would, however, be shattered
Stained beyond repair
The artist would have his sick fantasy displayed on every
shining surface
Yet only a monster such as this would take the longest
route to the hospital
Dragging every moment out
Giggling as another set of blades fall
A metal body melting
We're all just playing the floor is lava
And wherever the pale man has control is molten.

He is covered in crimson
Dripping on each step
Head tilted ever so slightly down
His hair sticking out in a dance of cowlicks
Twisted and standing
Smeared together with the air's ashes
Smirking as the wind lightly blows

A breezy walk to the northern part of town was doing him
some good
After all, how else would he stay in shape for a feast
And dress up for another one quite soon?

45

It's much too late for me to be watching this
As I turn off the tv I hear a whine
Both of them whimper in their sleep
Calmed only by a reassuring pat
Even though we all know they won't make it another week
I sit here sipping some freshly brewed tea
Trying to tell my nerves to sleep
Waiting for the meds to kick in
Praying for a restful sleep
Trying to ignore a restless issue.

The first to shatter was the children's hospital
The first to burn was the cancer hospital
A shame they have twin bridges connecting each other
Gasoline stains the ashy air
It was truly a beautiful sight
The tears of the innocence couldn't even quell the flames
Methodically I ensnared them in their rooms
Slithering through each office
Meeting some delectable people along the way
The secretaries were all lovely
But their glasses were a choking hazard

The doctors even patched me up
On threat of glorious execution
Retribution and revenge in scarlet wine
With cheese and grapes only missing toast.

Stroking their little heads
Lying in wait
Being lulled by the slow silencing of the two
Breathing becoming less strained
They were good natured
Although I fear that would be twisted
Contorted like a soul tormented in hellish infernal
nightmares
I fear for them with each passing night
One more might just be their last
The seas call me once more
Watching their dancing waves sway is a wonderful
pastime
Submerging me as I willingly take in a watery breath
Falling like the rare star on the blanket of the night.

It looks like some children found an escape
But the cancerous wicks burn like wildfire
I do hope they taste like crab
If only the labels fit
Drawing out another blade
I finish the job of the unwilling wicks
Tossing them like a fresh salad
Cutting into vegetables and baby cattle
The innocence burns to a crisp
Like pop rocks on a campfire

Just a little summertime fun in the fall
Single-handedly cleaning up the leaves on the once neat
streets
It's only now that we see
I haven't even begun yet
The night will become darker
Only becoming more grotesquely beautiful as time passes
Another night is all I ask
One more night or plenty
It's all the same to me
These streets will be painted and burned by these moonlit
hands
And that is a promise.

46

The hounds and I have become one
Hitchhiking off of my essence
They passed just to shift and warp
Contorting into twisted little devils
They stalk newly found streets
Our shared undying hunger will be quenched
Drunk off of the thought of another dose of ambrosia
Godhood held in its purest form
Covered in a lake of scarlet fluid and chunks
It's only a drop in the bucket
That's all each night is
Maybe one day I will replace the ocean
Making the swaying waves cured with cursed crimson
On the night that it all crumbles.

My crusade will only end when my rubies meet the pearly
gates
And make them crumble and decay
Just like a corpse of a few years
Maggots and worms all wriggle for the taste of sweet
rotten meat
All chewy, soft, and uncooked

Like a rare steak made by an incompetent chef
Only browned on the surface
With beauty found in vast juicy cheery cherry
All I can do is overdose on the delectable sanguine
Just as the fresh nights intended
The thirst grows exponentially by each passing moon
Becoming unbearable with the pale light's revival.

I will quench this land if I must
And gently float along with heads and kegs
Piercing dusty clouds of fluffy white
It's only right that my jet set eyes seek the finest of pearls
Nothing is too exquisitely expensive for my dear
Even dead she is worthy of gifts and praise
But it's truly that craving that makes me poke and prod
If I can't sleep then why should she
As selfish as that may be
Its unparalleled strength only adds to my own
All I have to do is let the night envelop me
And onwards I go
Towards the sweetest darkening skies
Lit only by the pure moonlight
Meeting my scarred babies' flesh and breathing life into
us.

47

We three lonely souls
Meeting in an inky communion
Stalking the fields and shifting through the corn
They found my sickly little hideout
My humble abode on an abandoned farm
Not too far from the dried station
If the gas wasn't depleted this field would be absent
A gory glory only serves to fuel the wildfire
I feel a kinship with the flames
We both desire sustenance for intensive and intrusive
hunger
Licking up warm wine furiously
Drunk off of the excitement of fading into the night
Spreading like ashes along the breeze
This everlasting relapse only burns brighter
Outshining ten moons yet fueled by a single orbital cheese
wheel.

I will soon be drunk
Like a farmer in the heat of a harvest
Waiting until the profits roll in
The sweat of a hard day's work sticks to my suit

The tatters and stains are all too much
And I realize in this mortal coil
I too have bounds
I have met them in the most aggravating way
Surrounded by the blues that shift and shake the wheat
Swaying in the light breeze
Lights shine on me
The heretics dare to mimic my precious moonlight
How dare they mock the eye with craters
It watches in silent horror as they surround me
The sun is rising, and it burns my eyes
I close them and let the internal dark take me
Being lifted and driven away
Unable to move but I feel and hear
Every little thing and minute detail.

They seek to cage me
Funnily enough, I think I'll play along
An excuse to rest before I bend the bars
Spreading flame to inmates and the blues
I think I will play this joke out
The hounds fled into the night
And like good little disciples will continue my work
Let us see how long they last
Without their leading head
Watching two betas fight for the power of bile and blight
To bark out orders and spread like a disease
We bring plague in spades of flame
But for now, I think I'll enjoy the ride
I do look forward to seeing that judge one more time.

48

I sit too far away from my precious barley and wheat
In the court playing a game
Of victimization and villainization
The foundry of this very civilization
The crops will go dry without me
To be honest it's better off this way
But if they aren't fed than I fear the nights alone
Like a dying old crow my concerns crow
The pair are the only ones that share the sin and hunger
with me
We are a bestial brotherhood betrothed to the night
Drinking the pale moonlight and dancing with the ashes
The old croon looks hesitant while the gabble is struck
As if he remembers the face of a crying man fifteen years
ago
In the same chair, in the same room
Even the same jury and month
It's our anniversary of sorts
But nobody noticed his shadow drop infernal venom into
his drink
The poor fool should have chosen water over coffee

His wife warned him, although I suppose she is his widow now
I do love how sickly fate can be.

Loaded on a cart
Saying goodbye to that old suit along the way
I'm off in orange to make another flame
The black was stained by ash after all
The white had spots of dirt
Plenty of holes and stitches too
I deserve much more dapper
Perhaps matching the rubies I hold so dearly
I will ascend to a jet-set status again
But for now, I want to see how far down I can go
Hopefully, the hounds understand
Although I can smell them along the breeze
I promise they will get the leftovers and scraps from my plate.

It's a slow crawl to the cells
And I slept comfortably
For a week I was sure to slumber through the poking and the prodding
The batons bashing into my side is a poor attempt to make someone wake
Yet a brutally real attempt to make someone strike back
Rising arms in a weak but raging flail
Soon I will rise out of this coffin they call a cell
And make this hell hole a fine tomb
Founded by ashes and flame
Justice served scorching

Burning the clouds that dare to strike back
I will start my reign from behind iron bars
But my steel is so much sharper and stronger
Molten, flexible, yet firm and wild like fire
Wouldn't you agree?

49

I think I will have a greet and meet tonight
To cook the rotten cattle
A gathering of hidden powder and herbs
To finally meet my dearest ground friend
Gunpowder and gasoline
But this time I will embrace the flames
The hounds have brought what I desire
Walking now on two feet
Adapting like a fish out of water
Slightly slouched and drooling
They are hungry with claws clinging to chunks of beef
Their eyes show much more flame than mine
And I lead them because of that
I control the burning and it whispers secret truths to me.

It starts out in small popping
Booms collide and combine along each cell
With all the sleepy faces showing an almost childlike calm
Resting their little heads before losing soap and the like in
the shower block
Not even their god will have mercy on their souls
Just as he had none for me

And now my cause is sweet and sour
Revenge that could rot a tooth
The screams of confusion ring through the erupting flames
I sit in the middle of it all
Gazing at the nighttime stars with my hounds
They have mutated beyond repair yet know their master
Resting their heads on my lap to a point where napping is
second nature
Watching the inferno slowly sink in a maddening laughter
Blocking out the whining and crying
Begging for a forgiveness they will never achieve
Even if it turns out I am a lowly servant of his mighty iron
grasp
I am a free agent and will take a throne
Even if the devil himself gets in my way
I will ascend to a cruel and brutal lord
But as his loyal hand
I only seek the power I rightfully deserve
Earned and paid for in the purest crimson food for an
army.

I miss the flames, but we will reunite soon enough
They were so much shorter than the last
But they blew each brick away and melted it all away
Letting the ash fly along the breeze
It's all so much better when cooked
A feast of filthy beef of the irredeemable and the few
pictures
Framed to an action they never would have dreamed of
They all will fall just the same
Goodnight to the fallen and bitter meat

For now, it's time to hunt for another suit
Orange is much too out of season
Perhaps it's time to fully delve and devour
Accept and feel
The crimson that calls my name.

50

A sense of dread lingers within me
Not only has the pale man been gone for more than a week
He has disappeared off the media
Except for the covered up prison burning
I drove there myself just to see the carnage
Although not much was left
Besides some bones, rubble, and burnt corpses
All meticulously placed in circles
Arms spread and holding hands
Staring into a sun they haven't been able to see.

Freedom by fire
The only suitable motto
With motives as jet set as silk
These rubies have shining glass drapes
Adjusting the sleeves slowly
This town has been tainted
The water is now blood
The bodies have been delicately placed
And yet nobody has come to investigate
All of them are too fearful of the monsters that stalk the woods

And like good cattle they listen to the hand with the prod
An electrifying example of what happens when they
disobey.

The house is cold and silent
It's both refreshing and terrifying
Each shadow makes me flinch
Every night I feel sick
I sleep more and more
Trying to escape the guilt
If he isn't here then Father is elsewhere
It's elsewhere that I'm fretting over.

The fabric is a perfect mix of comfort and stiffness
A crimson suit for the king of diamonds
Not as restrictive as the jet black I was encased in
Finally free to expose a shirt to match the internal pitch
As scarlet ties it all together
I finally picked the dirt and ashes out of my hair
Passable for some wealthy pale man
I will no longer be a corpse
But I will be in the court of them
Rotting away while I light the flame on just one more
night.

51

Out for another night on the town
A brisk walk to some stores
Window shopping while letting the hounds have their fill
Of the heads from newly silent corpses
If I'm getting a redesign then why shouldn't the dogs
Extensions of their master should dress as such
Two little bow ties and plates for the pale bones they
crunch
Almost like little butlers
One is black while the other is red
And through their waistcoats that color is seen
The skies dark grey covers their shirts
As they become more human
Like scrawny but powerful little dog men
Finely groomed and no one would be able to tell
Save for their faces
If they were man or something else
They are my little devilish partners after all
But they dare not question the alpha of the pack.

It's a lovely night for a midnight stroll
Watching as the cloud cloaks roll in
Taking the grand stage of the sky just to gift us with
sprinkles
A drop of moisture for the dying grass and ashes
It's just a divine tear
Dripping from the pearly gates
How could the world become so infernal?
How could the depths suddenly become not so deep?
Is humanity worth saving from the demonic champions it
creates
Or will it fester and die
Like a raisin drying in an agonizing demise
Set out in the sun by some irresponsible child
To be picked and eaten like an unwanted casserole
By some passerby pigeon
Looking for its next meal in a city of smog.

Only towers of smoke await its bitter end
Its beak becoming chipped as it crashes into the glass
Spiraling downwards as it's angelic wings finally fail it
Meeting once and for all with the vendor of a passing cart
Selling loosely named hotdogs to the street's scarlet
patrons
Foolishly ignoring the lessons of a forgotten Sinclaire
Just to watch as he is locked away and tormented for will
full ignorance
Daring to speak out against the system
Because it was meant to be wicked
There is no rest for those wolves
They meet with the workers in the same slums

Trying to escape the towers
Finding that the walls are all too tall
Giving up and returning to their jobs
Hammering away at the ground or their keyboards
Festering like pigs to the slaughter
Waiting to be replaced by a shinier gear
And then there are people like me
Who seek to liberate the pork from themselves
Although who doesn't like bacon from time to time?

52

This town is my mansion
And it being a mere walk away from my fields makes it
even better
I enjoy my plantation's throne
Although it is no fun working in it alone
Through all the infernal torment I push on these cattle
Could I push one over the edge to become like me?
More specifically
Could I keep it in the family tree?
Extend the roots to intermingle and warp
Turning the tree in stark black
With its gnarled fingers reaching to a sky it will never find
Not even flinching with the frigid breeze
Like shadows having a nighttime chit chat
That's a wonderful idea.

It's just another bloody night
And I'm beginning to fall for the smell
Flesh burning like a crisp leaf of an open flame
The sounds bring me back
To another breath
I'm enveloped in the pitch black sky

Yet it will never let me pierce through the clouds
Keeping me grounded in chains
But I climbed out of a cesspool before
So what's another one for the books.

The twins follow me
Like good little subservient jackal men
Shirking their duties to guard rusted gates
Finding contentment and joy
Or simply another meal
Enjoying the thrill of a positively burning hunt
It's a long walk home without a single regret
All eyes on us before their last gasp for precious air
But the smoke takes their lungs
As it fills my nostrils I feel alive again
The scent of an over glorified barbeque
And I just opened the smoker to see hanging meat
That slow roast will give it the juicy flavor I'm looking for
Just one more night is all I need.

53

It's midnight and I'm restless again
I'm home in bed hiding like a child failing to sleep
Fearful of the monster under his bed
But not the all-encompassing nighttime air the envelops
his sight
The knocking I heard an hour ago at my door that scares
me
Especially since the runes are still prevalent in the room
adjacent to mine
The slow crawl downstairs was the worst part
The stars in the sky were dim once more
But I knew the pale man was days away
I could feel it in my bones
As if it's an instinctual horror stemming from some
ongoing connection
Of which I know if impossible
And I both don't and won't have such a fearful feat under
my belt.

At the door
And much to my shock I find a pile of familiar books
My mind is racing

These all burned
I set the fire with my own hands
Who could have found them?
They haven't even a scratch on them
Although my notebooks were gone
The important information I kept for safekeeping
Hidden away to halt me from weeping
They returned to me like a stray puppy
All kept together with a band and a mortifying note.

Written in metallic scarlet
A simple phrase I do not want to read
Folded on the top but I can somewhat make out the words
Everything has come back with only a simple letter
With a shaking hand, I open it wistfully
Reading it out loud in disbelief and shock
"Your work isn't finished."
Marked by nobody in particular
Clearly meant for me and me alone
So I tote the books back and lock the door
Hiding from the problem now adjacent
Pouring the purple poison into me again
Dropping onto the messy nest I used to call a bed
Effectively knocking myself out
Letting the sea take me before I deal with the hurricane on
the horizon
And this time I can't flee.

54

It's back to the books I suppose
My paranoia settled like fine dusty powder
Although I may never know who truly got these books back
in my hands
My assumption is the seller
A maniac and a scholar
Laying hidden and docile in dusty tombs
He sells to the poor fools who seek knowledge
But no money changes hands
All he says is be careful what you wish for
And makes sure his customers learn even if they break
Forcing them to keep their word exemplified by the
madness of knowledge
Suddenly each day becomes marked
Unwanted eyes stalk the shady blots that dot every vision
Sight becomes a mixture of dream and skewed reality
Yet the eyes become more perceptive
Seeing through the haze of what we don't want to
understand
But the shellshock and screaming may not be worth it
As each step becomes haunted and louder

Pounding like the beating of a heart hidden under the
floorboards of the unsound
Slipping further and further
Some like myself trying to escape through flasks
Is it really fortunate to see like this?

Sight is a crow
Furiously pecking at a living scarecrow
Forced to dress in rags and hung
Rusty nails rammed through glistening palms
Crimson rolls and drips while more and more flesh is torn
Lacerated and eaten
It's the vultures now
A murder and committee working in perfect unison
Like twin Salem trials burning away at the stake
These eyes are knives that stab their holders
I behold blades digging into my flesh
All from words that shouldn't have been seen or translate
It's cursed speech in wicked tomes
It all floods back
The sea is no longer peaceful
Colliding with a horrible hurricane of wretched
proportions
Twisting and turning with the waves
The boat is being rocked and heading for a swarm
In unison they on a vomit green greedy squid-like bestial
undefinable mass
Ramming into a servant of the indifferent abyss
The captain went down with the ship and the crew
Unless it turns out he was alone the whole time

These eyes bring madness
One more night is one more curse
Pupils dilate and burn
Watch as they dash at the dancing words on the page
Hoping to find the final nail
In preparation of the coffin of an old life
Reborn only by letting the night swell in unaccepting veins
I can't be him and I never will be
No matter how warped I become
We both descended like fools
It's in our righteous blood
On a dead-set course for the crimson crusade
Unless we finally put our feet down
Braving the inky void and fleeing from madness
Until I finally find the nerve
To stab back.

55

The etchings don't keep me up as late as they used to
The runes are only freshened instead of carved
I'm slowly learning how to control a cursed sight
Hanging on to some form of hope
I will not descend again
Because it is not a question of whether I can or can't
It's a question of can I afford to
And the answer to that is a stark "no."

I'm knocking again
Although I sense a strange scent
A demon or abomination of unholy communion
It was here and at this very doorstep
But not one of violence and territory
It seeks not conquest but something more sinister
Perhaps even maddening to the mortal coil
But harmless nonetheless
The smell of a demon is his insignia
To others of the burning tormented ilk
It's secreted to show pride in the not so amiable actions
This is seen the most in the crusader's consequences

Smell echoes through time, based on the power of
prevalence
Leaving a permanent stain on mortals
And taking a nice percentage as them
Either convert or be enslaved
No greys in a system of ash and fire
Just a swirling way of going about life
And choices dancing in the stale air.

He walks in with gusto
Two familiar barking servants
Fresh clothing and groomed hair
Seemingly he spent the time to sculpt himself into a jet-set
redesign
Yet he sticks to his ways
Sleeping on the couch while the hounds curl up nearby
Except to accommodate for their mutated undying corpses
They sleep sitting up
It's only now that I realize the night is almost over
The sun may even poke out of the sky soon
Just like how I as the son creep out of the office door
Tomorrow schedules more work
But for today I will rest like them
Until the night calls me into its depths
And I see how deep the rabbit hole goes.

56

"Welcome to the world of dreams"
The bookseller told me as I took those tomes
They have become a tomb of sorts
Perhaps to lull me into an unshakable sleep
Although I didn't believe that lulling could be so agonizing
Suddenly when taking it all into your essence
Being warps and contorts like a giggling cloud crawling
out of a freezer
Makeup melting in the summer heat
A layer of frosty ice denigrating
Smiling as he becomes malleable
And just like the words that the bookseller told.

Is it malicious to curse someone with knowledge?
Or is it a drink that even the thirstiest of travellers would
drown via drop
We all think we know so much about the world
And each step is steady
Or that our species is somehow on top for a reason
That we can only progress with time
Yet we face a recession of thought
And try to hide from the truth

The world is much more wild, wicked, and weird than we think
And the reasons come from the stars or below
Because in the end, we are all minimal to the cosmic downfall
Or weak pawns on a war of horns and wings
We will be wiped out with the rest of them
Parallel to the livestock, we breed and capture
Why can't we accept we are just like them.

It's hard to look at the world through this cold indifference
Finding more and more ways to seek an end
Knowing is one thing
But understanding and taking it all into your being is a death wish
I think I have a wish
To be blind when this is all over
By my hand or the pale man's
Although I suspect I will be my own demise once again.

57

I think it's time to dispose of the rabble
I will make veal as the witnesses squeal
Gasoline has never been this putrid and bright
It's glorious to hear the feet stomping
People running into the shadow
Unaware that the shade beneath their feet can turn on them
Realizing all too late their own inky stain is forcing them
down
Crying and screaming in agony as it cuts into their
stomachs
The men, the women, and especially the children
Neatly cut into squares
A slow and grueling process for such a delicacy
All I can do is ask
Where's the beef in this tinfoil.

A rickety old building
Wood and bricks will become ash and rubble
The flames and I are hungry
And the hounds await their treat
Loyalty is in each of their breaths
Shirking an infernal duty

Out to dinner with a friend or two
The gates of hell needn't close
The blockage from the souls is already too much
The poor livestock live in a futureless futile world
And it's my job to get the most use out of the meat
As flesh is too flimsy for good clothing
My efforts are best suited in the kitchen
With blades and flame as my witness
I will feast tonight with my brothers
We will howl with the moons loving embrace
Bathing in pale moonlight
Just one more glorious night.

The crumbling is the best part
And like a burnt coffee cake the roof becomes powder
Ash and flame dance in rejoice
A mingling reunion of sorts
Silence settles in the rubble
Under rocks and ash, the veal is found
Cooked to a youthful perfection
Biting down on the chewy chunks serves a delicious flavor
I did these children a favor
Sparing them from a fate of memories
And in that, I have a blank slate
Starting over would be sweet if it wasn't more of the same
All I need is one more night
To make each movement less hollow
And make the world shake in scarlet shivering fear

Only one more night

And maybe then I can flee

And the pearly gates will know horrors of which it was previously spared.

58

On his return, I knew it spelled demise
The hounds haunted my footsteps
Watching expectantly until they drifted to sleep
Where I slipped away and studied again
Lights off but lit by candle
The pages flicker in the dim flame's gaze
Looks like these books have a scent too
And they want me to stop reading
I think I'll discover the sickening plot in the pale man's
skull
But for now, it's back to burning the midnight oils
This time I have a plan
A brother, not of blood but of water
I will selfishly divide the work I cannot do
Driving to his home we meet
It looks like these two colleges will stain their eyes
together for now
Birds of a feather do flock together
And we are those with sickened minds.

It's plagues like this
With the decadent taste of disease

That keeps us fools awake
One more night is another vial of blight
It's truly vile how deprived we can become
Just by seeking to know
Kicking and scratching every single edge
Desperately clawing to each word
And the runic letter haunt my dreams
Although its new color is melancholy
The scarlet and the flame has left my mind
The blur is now gentle
I am a cactus without thorns
Skillfully avoiding shadows with horns
Casting every word on my black tongue
As the chicken scratch multiplies night by night
Meanwhile, I sneak into the house to sleep
Six hours became four
Four becomes two
Hours become hooked to the pages
Wired to each word of the wicked wretched runic
nightmare of ink.

It's only now that I know how to cover my back
That the research takes an eerily silent tone
The curse of another night is less severe
The lack of seeking to sever a limb is refreshing
Although the problems are back
And my legs can't run fast enough
It's not nearly as rough as it once was
But one day
That will change.

59

Cheap liquor
A fitting gift for a slowly maturing Son
Barley living past a year of adulthood
My only wonder is what if my blood mingles with him
Will the anchor become a new weapon?
A Son to be proud of would help bring hell
Lacerations and carnage done by a family
The matron died with our sainthood after all
And those gates call for me to drop a match
Letting the gasoline rain
How is it I got this far
Without learning of such a gory surprise.

Cooking has never been something I have been good at
I like my steaks rare
And my stakes embedded in the loveless lingering
livestock
Rarely do I linger in the kitchen
But these dashes of wine and breadcrumbs call
A disguise on par with a jet black sky
Fresh veal from the mortal cows that stalk cities
And I will force this into his body

No matter how much bile burst from the belligerent boy
Father knows best after all
I just want my son in on the family business
He will grow up just like his old man
And pride will be a crown for me to gift him.

The grease pouring out of the pots and pans
Echoes a successful frying
As out of character as it may be
This well-cooked food matches my well-groomed exterior
A new taste in fashion and wealth
As well as delicacies in food
An ancient set of cheap china is placed
And as he comes home I smile
My dearest Son
Will make daddy proud
By embracing a sickening lifestyle of fine wine and nights
jet set in pitch black and blight.

The servants sit at the table
A rounded little bug ever so slightly too short for the
chairs
A cross inverted with people as points
The nightly affairs of a knight to pick a loyal squire
Even if I have to do it by knife
My precious carvers have perfected edges
Sharp enough to cut through bone
Cleaned from the rusting blood
Iron's ills won't infect my steel
But the parasite will move in for the kill
So somebody can comprehend every star in a starless sky.

60

A demon's dinner is disgusting
And as my body rejects it
My neck is pushed into the table
A shade being willed by a pale man
Clad in crimson and an apron
The kiss in "kiss the cook" is scratched out by sharpie
"Obey the cook" is staining my eyes
As my bile drowns me in disgusting meat
The grease burns my eyes
As tears roll down and the light leaves me.

Too much for him
Or at least I assume
I succeeded in tainting his blood
The mortal meat mixed with demon's blood
Dinner was quite simply a splendid success
His days are numbered
And I will gain a Son to be proud of
For now, I toss the apron aside and head for gold
Skulls crack by the force of a club
Spiraling into the pale moonlight
Entertainment by pearly bones

Just give me one more night
And I will reach those over glorified cloudy gates
That gaudy cream color stains my eyelids
I can feel the cotton in my palms
And my thorns are stronger than its.

The sea has taken me
But now the waves are violent
A scarlet sea rushed back to where is parted
And it's my part to drown while the herd is shepherded
away
I can feel my pupils shifting and shaking
Eyelids fluttering but staying shut
Jerking limbs in a harming disarray of silent screams
I awaken with empty lungs
My pounding head burns me in the morning
The mirror shows a little more crimson in my eyes
And as a victim of a wicked crusade
My blood boils in its own wicked blight
I am stained by the night
But I will not become one of its children
Or at least, that's what I promise.

61

One more night
Dead set on another kill
Prey lays in wait
Oh dear
I'm stalking it on its long thin legs
Swaying with the midnight breeze
Wrapped in twilight arms
A cold and distant embrace
As my claws rake down on their backs
Their shades turn against them
From bleak to beautiful crimson
Scarlett pools with a sweet taste
All I'm doing is cleaning house
Wares used to be here
But now they lay on meat hooks
Looks like the butcher will have to wait for his shipment
These sheets of sharp steel will keep me comfy
Lined on the ground
Examined one by one
Just to be thrown and embedded into a firm skull
Crackling like pixie dust

I lay here cackling
A cold grey floor
Concretely mine for now
It was abandoned yet shipments ran through
Black goods for cheap in these markets
If its illegally theirs
Its rightful mine
I make a throne of chalky bone
Clinging together through dripping flesh
The inferno calls back at me
Clinging to the shadows I stole and rising.

Soon enough I will find my crown
My heir will be worthy of a throne of his own
Air will come back into my dusty lungs
And I will grasp on pearly bars
Chalky white will break down shining streets
Diamond lamps will shatter with a red sea's breeze
Let's stain these clouds red
Draped in pitch of the night
The sky calls with the moon
And it would be a shame if I didn't answer.

62

The sun burns
It brings me to a boil
Blight and turmoil meet me on its crisp waves
Yellow and orange dance on my skin
Like an infernal daydream turned nightmare
Worsening every day like a plague
The clock is ticking
Tocking tells me I'm running out of time
Yet a need for rest is leaving
Wired on blood's wicked flame
What have I become?

Books don't warp me anymore
But they do still hide away their secrets
Yet the runic writing now filters like clear water
Every meaning and each stroke's purpose
Just a pulsating heart above each word
I breathe them inside of my blackening lungs
With the taste of cheap cigarette
Lighting a candle with a dirty herb

Trying to smoke my worries out of a paper finger
Letting each restless night float away and stain the air
Being swept away with a rare burst of breeze.

Knowledge has poured into my veins
And as my eyes flash in scarlet envy
I wish for the green of an ignorant field to return
Although it was never truly green, was it
Intermingling with the blue of a cursed branch
And now the pale man is a storm of his own
From charred twig to horrific hurricane
Tearing through homes
Splitting more families than a slave trade
Except with no chance of survival
A cursed life lived through cursed eyes
Cured of any ignorance
Poisoned with a miserable scholarly vile
Bile of which has haunted us for centuries
Do humans truly want the knowledge we seek?
If knowing is burning
With the way things are going
We will burn with either way
Living in this stagnant cave of blue swirls.

63

It's a bitter thought
The ones where we realize
We have found isolation in a world of interlocking conflict
And yet it's been stained by our inherent need to be as one
Yet individuals with similar simplicity
Could we all learn to smile
While the family dog whimpers
Dying in the arms of its youngest master
Just like this cursed hound
As it rests its head on my lap
Setting the silver tray aside
Just wanted a bedtime story
The heads were never meant to last
Another sick means to an end
Twisting the result to a beautiful gory glorious
slaughterhouse
The cave should have crimson pools as oceans
After all, it where it all started.

It's funny how a demon sees a genesis
Wanting to go back to the garden
Play a trick on the test subjects

But this time widening
Let us all eat the poisoned fruit
Truly let us feel the excruciating demise that awaits us
As flames twist and twirl
Eating up even the air in a greedy lust
The brand of which stems from a horrible deed
But doing it anyway
All out of a misplaced pleasure
There is no money or fame in this
Sick and twisted like a clown shoved in a freezer
Hearing chunks move back into place as he contorts
Crawling out with stains of scarlet
Just one more night until the fool with a red nose is put out
Like a flame on a candle
But first, we must burn the moth.

Is it only nature that drives us to flame?
Or is it a hidden need
To blaze a trail or die trying
Dying dirt roads red
Bathing in it's deepening the pool
Chugging the Kool-Aid of a plague's frenzy
Dipped like a strawberry in chocolate
And devoured by the blaze and its embers
Becoming one with the ash that irritates the eyes of the
fallen
Wandering like a stray
Lost and alone
Dwindling away with the lack of food
Providing a blank slate
While the pale man stalks the pearly gates.

64

The smell of cheap meat
A chunky crimson stew
Slowly boiled to perfection
The fruit of a corrupted crusade
Scarlett lines the rusty walls
It's here I find my calling
I won't be needing these servants for too much longer
Although their lives were shortened
None will usurp the throne I seek.

My home is found among hooks
These fish will be hung for display
Precious scales that hide juicy flesh
Skinned to perfection and blood drips like rain
Trickling into basins
All hoisted into the air
Draining into the next layer of collection
I am greedier than an army of diseased mosquitoes
But this throne won't build itself
Blood money is energy
Each breath is blessed by the pitch blanket
Wielding a harsh curved blade in the sky

Yet it remains dull
Unlike these carvers that I wield
Decorated and designed but never for use
These ruby handled weak blades will surely shatter
But the trusty carvers remain as the backup
I am a general in an army of steel
And they all listen until the breaking point
Finding solace in a slippery scarlet demise.

Giggling in a day that can't burn me
I have rested enough
The harvest season is a new dawn
That I will conquer with the coming moon
Cities watching the skylines in anguish
Rubble in awe at a sky's indifference
While rats scuttle along the streets
And livestock meets plague of which it's never seen
The pitch black cloak falls upon me
Skin as pale as bones
Dead set on finishing this crusade
The gates will behold terror of which it couldn't have
conceived
And I will grasp the crumbling bars
Onwards to a new era.

65

It's nights like these I ponder
With him gone and the hounds around me
Stalking me like an eerie group of shadows
Yet whimpering in their uneasy sleep
Are like their lives slowly draining
Or they will be further warped?
One got impressively more violet
I am not the alpha to them
But this one will be punished in time
For now, I skim these pages
As runic crimson floats to me
And I learn more than I bargained for.

From naught but a farmer dabbling in art
To an industrialist manufacturer
Letting clunky machines run themselves
A factory all for me
Basins draining and wires tied and tried around
Hanging beef is stagnant in dead air
The smell is intoxicatingly toxic
A wonderful piece of land
As cheap plastic tubes are put to the test

Stained red with these unshaking scarlet hands
Blood running like a flood
These contraptions are more than enough
But watching as every drop drains from skinned faces
Is truly a sight to behold
As their eyes dry out
And another shipment comes through.

Control feels like an uphill battle
His plague has begun its true purpose
To take over the flimsy host
I will become like the hounds
If I sit here and wait
Letting the days slip further and further
A lust for blood echoes in my tainted mind
And I fear the day these hands will be stained
Unless I begin a hunt
But are these hands strong enough
To murder the Cerberus that stalks this world.

My servants will soon learn
There is no place for them
And the heir will lose everything if he dares step out of
line
My son should know better than to cross my shining
scarlet palms
But we both know that a cross fits uneasily in his hands
Shaking in the wind like a leaf
A backbone will be bestowed on his weakness

I will not have a weak link as an heir to my kingdom of ash
But for now, I have to find the people closest to the young wimp of a Son
Perhaps an even an informal scholar.

66

I shadow the hounds
Like a hunter stalking gazelles
Through this scope, I can see the meaning behind glass
eyes
Starless like the night sky
They are humble servants
Husks of hounds turned mutant men
Pawns of the cruelest sort
Why kill the enemy king
When you can have him under your thumb
After all, two royal vaults are better than one
Wealth in knowledge and blood
But little does he know
How weakened his pawns really are.

Sharpening wood
Distracting the hounds with steaks
A cheaper armory than most
Stakes of varying sizes
Hidden inside of a thin jacket
The fall air becomes damp

As I dry off one hound detects the treachery I have
committed
Five vials depleted to four
A holy method of cooking
Running into the bathroom in an attempt to vomit the bile
away
While the other hound stays oblivious
Tinkering with its scarlet tie
Licking its lips and watching expectantly.

The plan is going without a hitch
No going back now
I will burn this pitch-black fantasy
But staring into those glassy eyes
I see more than hunger
Gazing further into the pools I see myself
Becoming more of a shell
Trying to put an end to this forced transformation
This is where I put my foot down
I will waste one more night
My nerve may be weak
But tapping into this plague will bring a drop of the pale
man into me
And I will abuse that wicked detail
Just wait and see.

67

Strolling into the bathroom
Where fur is matted down
Vile, bile, blood, and more
All swimming in a draining bowl
Where bowels are dumped
And towels are thrown around
I pat his back once
Before turning to close the door
Feeling scarlet enter my eyes
White runs red in ravenous revenge
Grabbing the flimsy oak
And piercing his back.

Unable to howl with the projectile bile stemming from a
burning stomach
I press his head further into the ruined water
Breaking his snout in the bowel bowl
Making each drop spilled fill his cursed lungs
Rapid flailing is doing him no favors
And once I stop I remain
Not fooled by an act of unconscious
With a free hand, I put pressure on the cheap metal

The chunky liquid swirls and bubbles
Holy and unholy mingle
Acidic to the touch
A gory display of swirling
Suddenly it all stops and fill with more water.

The clogging wasn't all too surprising
But lifting the hound's skull was
With broken bones retracting into the skull
Bloodied and beaten to a fine pulp
Empty eyes speak a tale of the damned
Wide-eyed and staring back at me
As the plunger delves into the acid
It melts away as it moves above the seat
Yet it manages to flush this time
Leaving a burn in the bowl
As I roll the body in a rug and its towels
And toss it into the shower
There is no going back, is there?

68

He stepped out of line
And he will learn to respect my dripping hands
Or else his little friend will suffer at them
I have found him by the musty scent of old books
Sitting on his roof and waiting
Waiting for a car to buzz into this driveway
Before I steal him from his life
I may even toy with him in the workshop
Tinkering with such terrible machinery
Should lead to some fun
All I seek is to paint the night in a scarlet fury
Is that really too much to ask?

The glass is flimsy
Shattering like cheap plastic
I smell mouse
I'm hoping we play a good game
With me as the cat
Before I take him to the hooks
Make an example out of him
Martyrdom is a lie that he won't have the pleasure of
taking

Yet I would love to see that head roll
Go to the lanes for a nice bowl
Watching as the lopsided fleshy bowling ball stops dead in
its tracks
Laughing at the trail of light crimson
As a maggot pops out an eye
With a gaping mouth torn to shreds.

Fleshy bits and scarlet
Pink tattered like weak cloth
Blood drains from the rat's face
As a clatter tells him to fall
A bump on the side of his head
What a pitiful end
But I think I will delay it
This young pup is lucky to have my pity
Patience is a virtue
And all I need is one more night.

69

The splinters fly into my face like agitated rain
I grasp wildly into my jacket
Choppy wooden knives can save me
Or so I hoped
The hound was poisoned after all
And as the brutish butler stood over me with darkened
eyes
Our black met in a dizzying stare
And something whispered to me
Primal, bestial, and almost demonic
I would be foolish if I fought both
I thought to pick the lesser evil
Being submerged in the addictive scarlet fury of a
thousand starless nights
My life drowning in a red sea
These hands will serve the crimson fluid
For one night only.

Darting forward in a blind charge
Bashing the dog out of my way
Skipping through the slim hallway
I waited in the living room

The bullish hound rammed into my chest
As I pierced his back with a righteous strike
Tearing into the stomach and slowly teasing the splintery
wood
The more his teeth sunk the more I spun out of his grasp
Producing another from the light fleece
No longer white with no hopes of repair
Laughing as I forced a stake through his hungry eyes
Extinguishing a flame with naught but blood
Dancing around the furniture in a delightful blur
Drunk off of the lust of an Aztec god
Waiting to sink my teeth into a nice chunk of meat.

A jump and a skip
Bouncing off the walls in a caffeinated ballet
Lacing the hound in the tattered jacked
Wood lacerating flesh like a grotesque movie
Where the protagonist sinks into a rage among the
bloodsuckers
Except I will not leave any ashes
Perhaps I went too far
Nine stakes all sunk in rows of blood
Stomach acid hitting the floor
His tongue drops out of his wounded snout
As blood drips from mouth and nose
I grab his neck and tear with ungodly strength
My bare hand managed to rip off his skull
The loose hanging flesh gained from a satisfying tear
Just like papier-mâché
Except satisfyingly scarlet

And as I sank from my high
The reality of the what the red pill did hits me
As I sink into the horrors of a blue one.

70

Hunger hits me like an atomic bomb
The crimson seeks to consume me
To court me into a forced marriage
And to consummate our vows in red
Throwing away soft white and lace
To chase me with whips and chains
Unless I buckle my knees
But that is the one thing I cannot afford.

Dragging a limp body for miles is easy
When he is slumped on your back and you move through
the trees
Like a spastic ape caffeinated on a midnight drug
A capsule always under my tongue
Making my eyes dazzle with wretched stars
I stole the sparkles from the pitch black blanket
And as it's not so humble servant
I reserve to right to the world it watches
And I will find those gaudy pearly gates
Just to watch them bend and twist
The crimson of this crusade burns into my palms

And I am gracious enough to gift it to those stuck up
chickens
Just as I have to the cows.

With my scraps of consciousness, I flee
Locking myself in the dank basement
Cooling off in its almost endless void
Throwing the key as far as I can
Shaking away in the corner
Desperately grabbing my knees as I twitch
The inhuman torment takes me
As my limbs jut and spasm
I twist and contort like a broken ragdoll
In the hands of a cruel child
Wanting nothing more than mommy's warm embrace
But more so the money stashed in her wallet
To steal away in the night on a binge
Rewarding himself with awful behavior
And still expecting to be coddled
Still demanding to be coddled.

71

Emerging from the whetted void
More concrete than the inky black's floor
The only hunger I feel is that of a mortal man
Easily solved with leftover chicken
Kentucky fried never tasted this good
The mess of nights prior remains
In truth, I have no idea on how long I was hiding
The shaking didn't let me get sleep
And the dreamless limbo looked just like the room in
which I resided
Looking towards the living room
The only thing upright was a small circular table
Its rounded and smoothed edge were battered shards
But it had enough room for the small package on top of it.

I opened the box
The smell of overpriced cologne rolled off of it
Knowing who this was from I hesitated
Then carefully moved the cardboard to reveal a shock
A simple handgun
Stainless. unused. empty.
As if it was fresh from the store

It glistened, beckoning me to pick it up
My hand slowly grasped its leather grip
A note was taped to the other side
It said simply, "You're grounded."

Examining the box lead to nothing
Moving it revealed a horrific realization
A simple polaroid of a familiar figure
Bloodied and beaten
Bruised beyond repair
Hanged by his arms on rusty meat hooks
An address is written in smeared black across the right side
Then suddenly everything clicked
Just like the barrel of this gun soon will.
This is my only promise.

72

Like Father like Son
My wife always hoped
When breath still flowed from her pale face
Smiling at me with that beautiful grin
One of the few genuine graces in my life
Now I am here
A gory mess of glory
But does a beast truly regret its hunger
Or is it just me regretfully falling from my high?
I miss my graces
The bloody, the damned
And the lovely late night dancing.

Those days are far gone
Almost sixteen years since it all ended
My anniversary of sweet death is nearing
And I want to make it special
By proving my love right after all of this time
My boy will be something to be proud of
But it will still be my hands to pry those gates out of the
sky
Never question why I have stopped this far

It was fated by the hand that sent me down
Deep into a burning crust
Giving me passion inside purpose
Knowing I have always been purposeless
Until the day I crawled from that grave
My skin is still as pale
Only a year and so much was done.

Oh, to hell with it all
I will make this world shake
My craving will be quenched
It won't make a difference to the rat
Barely hanging onto life
I guarantee he will lavish in the pity I will bestow on him
Cravings will be quenched
My teeth will sink into that fine steak
And my son will be none the wiser.

73

I dug it up just like I buried him
Except I can look upon this single object with pleasure
And a desire to quench my thirst
The layer of rust on this lead is still smooth
Almost divine in the way it tingles my skin
Although the water did sting
Placing it into the chamber and clutching the gun with
both hands
I have one shot
And I wish it could be destined towards me.

The crawl to the car
Then a long drive
That warehouse is a well-known spot
Where teens would gather before it was taken over
Cartel territory with shady dealings
Hard to believe there was a local black market
I still remember exploring that place
Nature was beginning to take it in my youth
The light from broken windows was perfect
Proportions and positions
Like spotlights on a grand stage

Turned wicked by one cruel man
The night will not protect him this time
He will burn for damning my soul
And this time he won't come back.

When I saw the note it all hit me
I have a single chance to end the pale man
And with that
A chance to save me from becoming his heir
I will not take up his new found family business
And I would much rather see his estate burn
Even if it has to die with me
One shot left for damnation or salvation
Just need to keep putting pressure on the gas
Mile by mile it comes closer
My nerve can't afford to falter just as I can't afford to get
caught
But the difference between me and my dear Father
Is quite simply, I won't be caught red-handed
As a gun's smoke doesn't leave a trail in flames
And being flashy just isn't my nature.

74

He was a tasty meal
And as time ticks I know my son will find me here
Holding a corpse smeared in blood
But perhaps I should dress the rat
Even after I tore some precious meat, he is alive
I say bandages and a coffin
A little grave outside
Lying dead in a hole
I am a hound, and this is my kill
Yet I am the master
The knives fall in my hands
The amount of shattered steel
Bend scrap metal
All beautifully displayed in a mosaic collage
It spells hell in its purest element
Cold and steady yet bloodied and rusty.

The rat was easy to wrap in a musty burrito
I am here on a throne of bones
All I can do is rise
These corpses are on display for an heir
As Father, I will pass this estate

After all the mortal world is best left to a mortal
The transformation is only complete
When he fully accepts the devil inside of him ·
Or makes one of himself
My son will do me proud
Whether he knows it or not.

With all this time I have spent
Each drop of scarlet glory
Every screaming soul echoing in my eardrums like a
symphony
One more night and it will all end
I will reunite with my love
With the new love, I cannot ignore
The taste for blood and blazing a trail
I can see the gates when I blink
One more night
And this crusade will end
The throne calls, and it would be a shame if I left her
waiting.

75

I roll up under the watchful eye of the moon
Its face usually full of glowing craters
Grotesque giggling emerges from creaky doors
Slightly open and moving with the breeze
A hole in the ground grumbles as I approach
And my old friend is wrapped in a cocoon
Yet I feel indifferent
Like a God to his creations
Knowing that the dead are dead
It's out of my hands now.

Laying on my throne
Legs cradled off of the right side
Lazily resting my head on my knuckles
I await this meeting
The blood in his veins is too weak to the vile
My bile's pure acidity could boil the strongest
I learned from the best of serpents
And not only that
I cursed him with knowledge
And with that, he should know
The curtains are calling.

My wounds remain undressed
Only a tattered and stained white shirt clings to me
Sweat, blood, and tears
The bags under my eyes only get heavier
But I will put an end to it all
One bullet, it's either him or me
At this point, I don't even care what it's going to be
The pale man will go back to the realm of the damned
A hellish fate awaits the both of us
But if I'm going down then so is he
Like Son like Father
His awakening will be in flames.

The end is near
Yet it's been quite a ride
As I slowly rise and clap
I smile and calmly walk forth
He has the gun clutched to his side
My son is too weak to shoot
The final stage of his turning will begin
The night will take over
And whisper to us
The final orders for this crusade
I lead and yet was led
A hero of this crimson war
I raise my flag and creed up high
As the moon turns scarlet with my eyes.

The pale man beckons me
Our eyes meet in a crimson stare
Only silence

The kind that gives way to a choice
Severe consequences await
Yet I know how disposable I am
I don't need to live in this world after I pull the trigger
Runic etchings float in the air
Glowing and dancing around us
First, it was separate cylinders
Then as he touched my shoulders they collided
A burning flurry staining my eyes.

The transformation is going swimmingly
These runes will make the crimson fluid his own
My bile will mutate into his
I pass on this gift to him
In hopes, he takes the throne of bone with an iron grip
Ruling a world of livestock
There is no other night
Tonight I let my anchor become his own
I bestow freedom upon his crimson eyes
Yet it's a shade darker than mine
And so much more focused.

My head bobs down in my exhausted haze
Shaking my head, I look into his eyes once more
I will accept his legacy of crusade
Only to end it as we stand here
My hand raises and he grins
*Almost amused by a mortal weapon being wielded against
him*
*I will never forget the sight of the light fading from his
eyes*

A bullet through the center of his forehead
A jolt of shocking blood
Then the sweet lull of death
There is no warmer embrace than the inferno
As the moon disappears behind clouds in shame
We both lose our red
And a fog of ashen pitch rolls in.

76

I collapse onto the ground
It's finally over
How I wish it had never occurred
This godforsaken crusade
As I wipe the dirt from my face
The cocoon groans from the pit
I crawl over and see his eyes open
Hearing his last words reminded me of it all
I lost everyone I loved
And numb indifference has taken me
Broken me like an archaic record.

Today was the anniversary
Of when he crawled from the grave
I remember seeing it on the news
The shock of a corpse missing
Exemplified by it being my own Father
I never expect him to be so sick and twisted
Nor did I expect him to sabotage my soul
The hounds lay dead in my home
Only two reasons left to live now

Rising with creaky bones of youth
I pop the trunk and grab the first container of gasoline
It is fire's ale after all
And it should be treated as such with this alcoholic match
The sloshing becomes rhythmic
As time ticks away
The match slips from my fingers
But this time I watch the flame I produced
Standing by its eerie warmth
At least for a little while.

It's almost like I arrived home instantly
Every action is now a blur
And as I crack open another drink
And doused my childhood in gasoline
I set the books aside
In a simple trunk with a note for the bookseller
And as the sun rises
I drive until I hit the hospital two towns away
As the inky void washes me out to an unconscious sea
I wonder, where do I go from here?

www.ingramcontent.com/pod-product-compliance
Lightning Source LLC
Chambersburg PA
CBHW061945070426
42450CB00007BA/1053